To our mother, Clarice Tilchen, a woman with extraordinary courage, strength of character, and compelling wisdom. Life is the preeminent teacher, and our mom, a superior student.

Sharon Tilchen Balaban and Mark Tilchen

Contents

Foreword: Mom
Acknowledgements
Introduction

Chapter One	Anna Glassberg	1
Chapter Two	Life Goes On	7
Chapter Three	The Lonely Years	13
Chapter Four	The Family	21
Chapter Five	The Great Tragedy	25
Chapter Six	The Pride of Judea	31
Chapter Seven	Dream World	37
Chapter Eight	My First Job	43
Chapter Nine	Life At Home	49
Chapter Ten	From a House to a Shoe Box	53
Chapter Eleven	Making New Friends	55
Chapter Twelve	Nightmares and Visions	59
Chapter Thirteen	Nat's Tales	65
Chapter Fourteen	A Voice from the Grave	69
Chapter Fifteen	Married Life	75
Chapter Sixteen	Deepdale Gardens	83
Chapter Seventeen	Changing Jobs	97
Chapter Eighteen	A Dream Wedding	115
Chapter Nineteen	Sharing with Shirley	121
Chapter Twenty	Cancer - - Again and Again	133

The Final Chapter   141
Epilogue   143
About the Authors   149

Foreword: Mom

Sharon Tilchen Balaban, daughter:
I remember asking Mom to tell me stories of her childhood and life in the orphanage, suggesting that she record the experiences. She said she would write it down, short stories turning into longer drafts, and eventually a book. The initial intent had not been to tell her story to the world, but to connect her life and experiences on paper as a documentation and reference for our family in the future. Perhaps releasing the burden would be a positive step in her personal growth. Growing up, the family, her kids included, knew snippets, and we perceived this extraordinary woman as content yet disheartened. We realized she concealed a complicated and darkened past. The relationship with her sister burdensome and her marriage conflicted, and yet she dearly loved both her sibling and husband.

Having offered the suggestion of a tape recorder, Mom said, "I could never talk into one of those things." After rejecting the idea of a recording, she took to pencil and paper, writing and rewriting a lot. These stories did not begin as a book but Mom became extremely excited once she got started. No one knew at the time about her writing and she did so for months, memories time can never erase flowing to sheets of paper.

Mark Tilchen, son:
I remember as far back as age five, waking in the middle of the night to discover Mom working; a seamstress, altering other people's clothing for a few extra dollars when her kids required something or additional money for the countless family road trips.

When her birthday arrived Dad frequently gave cash. That seemed to be her favorite gift. Unlike an article of clothing or something personal, money had genuine value and inevitably new outfits for Sharon and me – never anything for herself.

At a family gathering, the adult conversation had turned to growing older and having grandchildren. "I will never have children," words blurted from this young ten-year old mouth. Of course the aunts and uncles offered assurances one day I would. After all, what does a ten year old know about having offspring.

This had little to do with not liking children, since I happened to be one. Mom devoted her existence to her kids. What we ultimately became had been embedded upon us through her. Yes even at ten, it seemed impossible for one person to devote so much to children as my mother had done, and I had no plans to follow in her footsteps.

My life as a balloon, floating on the air currents, traveling the world, a story about a summer vacation written for a school report, brought enormous praise from a teacher, with Mom suggesting I pursue a career in journalism. Looking into this idea it became apparent despite fine creative thoughts, a journalist had to be outgoing. Although inheriting the desire for exploration from Mom, she also bestowed her introverted personality. Remembering my mother's encouragement to live creatively, here I am using those skills to edit her autobiography.

On reading Mom's journal I can finally appreciate why this woman lived her life the way she did. *Blame it on Anna* is Mom's words (with some light editing for clarification and grammatical repairs). Sharon and I offer our perspective in the expectation the reader will recognize that hers was not a life of misfortune, but of triumph. Our point of view is indented; provided at the end of a chapter as appropriate.

Sharon and Mark:
Widely used by our parents and relatives because of their European connection, Yiddish, which means Jewish, is a language spoken by Jews in Eastern and Central Europe before World War II. Yiddish is derived from German with words from Hebrew as well as other languages and is spoken in Israel, the United States, and Russia. We heard Yiddish phrases tossed in with family conversations as we grew up, but never picked up the language ourselves.

And so the story begins…

Dos leben iz di gresteh metsieh. Men krigt es umzist.

Life is the greatest bargain. You get it for nothing

Acknowledgments

Clarice Tilchen:
To my brother and sister-in-law, Arthur and Ilene, instrumental in helping me along the road of improvement and progress. To my daughter, Sharon Balaban, who encouraged me to put the true story of my life into words. Without her love and support, this book never would have been written. To son-in-law Joel Balaban, always there with an encouraging word when things got tough and I was nearly ready to give up. To my son, Mark Tilchen, who always said, "Keep trying and it will work for you."

To respected cardiologist Dr. Bob Dresdale, who regularly monitored my physical health so I might stay strong and have the ability to write about my life - which I felt so strongly about. To Dr. Martin Agan, respected psychologist, who helped me gain mental freedom so I could continue to grow and make my dreams a reality. To Jacqueline Gallagher, who carefully took the time to modify, correct, and organize this story, turning it into a structured and cohesive manuscript.

Finally, to all the doctors, nurses, hospitals, and others who played such a fundamental part in my life - you know who you are. Thank you all!

Sharon Tilchen Balaban and Mark Tilchen:
Thank you to Cousin Arlene, who helped us recall some of the details of our mother's life and to Cousin Ellen for her thoughts on her father and assistance with photos. To Stan Friedland, President of the Pride of Judea Alumni, and Dr. Paul Hirsch, Pride of Judea historian, for assistance with photographs. Dr. Friedland is the author of, *An Orphan Has Many Parents*, an excellent chronicle of the Pride of Judea (KTAV Publishing House, Nov. 1998).

Introduction

Clarice Tilchen:
This is a true story. For the earlier part of the book I had to rely on recollections told to me by my mother. I lived the rest. The names and locations have not been changed. It is the story of the arranged marriage of my mother, Anna Glassberg, the unhappiness this caused for her as well as for her family, and of an eventual mental breakdown. It tells of the misery that led her to try to kill her husband as well as herself. And of course, the terrible effect on me and my brother and sister. Through it all the three of us struggled to make the best of things for ourselves as well as for our families.

Today, at 71, I am proud to say that I've made it through what at times seemed like an impossible life. I am a changed person and my hardships have made me stronger than I ever thought I could be.

Chapter One
Anna Glassberg

In 1905, Grandpa Max and Grandma Sara Glassberg came to America from Russia with eight young children - four boys and four girls. The boys were Murray, Arthur, Bernie, and Irving; the girls named Ray, Mollie, Anna, and Rose. The family settled in Brooklyn in New York City.

Grandpa, a builder, and with money to be made in America, in short time owned a number of apartment houses and life became quite comfortable. Everyone in the family wore fashionable clothing and lived in a tastefully but expensively decorated apartment. They possessed every appliance available – radio, wind-up Victrola - you name it and they owned it. Grandpa would have nothing but the best and was very good at spending money.

Max generally had a good nature, but he remained strict with the children - to keep them in line! Even so, he had their love and respect. Grandpa, handsome and confident, walked proudly, always with his head held high, so proud of himself and of his family, and happiness and contentment radiated on his face. Grandpa had thin brown hair and a small bushy mustache with deep brown eyes that twinkled as he smiled. Pretty, with long, thin, brown hair pulled back into a tight bun, Grandma was soft-spoken and exceptionally shy.

The daughters attended school until the fourth grade while the boys on the other hand, all finished college. Back then people understood a woman's place was in the home. She needed to learn how to cook, clean, sew, and bake so one day she would make some gentleman a fine wife and be a good mother to her future children. Boys required an education, for they must learn how to make a first-rate livelihood to support their families.

But Anna, my mother, longed for an education. Oh how she loved to write stories and poems. In spite of her perfect English she knew her wishes would never be fulfilled. Rose taught herself to play the piano and years later took lessons. Little did she know that one day she would become a teacher and earn a living this way.

The children all grew to be fine ladies and gentlemen – friendly, outgoing, and fun. That is, with the exception of Anna, more akin to her mother - shy, quiet, and introverted. Anna's sisters often took advantage of her, stealing her underwear and blouses and wearing them when their own became dirty. Although Anna squealed on them to her parents, they rarely did anything to change the behavior. Anna became the scapegoat and surely the sisters had been envious of her. The prettiest of the four, Anna could never stand up for herself and so the behavior continued. Her siblings, the most important people in her life, were her life. She loved them dearly and felt they could do no wrong and so she always forgave them.

Ray, the eldest of the children, had a boyfriend named Nat, tall and exceptionally handsome, a shoe salesman who made a decent living and years later became a coffin salesman. As a teenager, Anna dated a boy, a small-time actor, though Grandma and Grandpa were not happy with either match and tried to break them up with no success. The girls would sneak out whenever they could.

A few months went by and Grandpa met Max Licht, an expert tailor from Russia who at a young age had also come to America with his parents and younger brother. Max spoke excellent English, but preferred Yiddish and used it often. Though short, round, and chubby, he was considered a good catch and his face actually quite handsome.

Max had started a dress-making business in the basement of his home (more closely resembling a cellar - dingy and unpainted with dim lighting). In one corner sat a mound of coal for the nearby boiler used for heating the house and for hot water. The rear area had been arranged with sewing machines, an ironing board, cutting table, shears, and shelves lined with thread of every color. The irons, made of a very heavy cast iron metal, were heated by a small electric burner, and worked on pulleys. Max owned needles, pins, razors, and other such equipment a tailor required to operate a successful business. Near the sewing machine he used most often, Max had a small window looking out to the backyard. And a thriving business it was - he made quite a good living.

Tailoring his night work, during the day Max had a job working in Manhattan in the garment district. He did not own a car and traveled by subway, a five-block walk from his house to the station. Max was very jolly and his whole belly shook when he laughed. Quite talkative, he constantly had a story to tell or a song to sing.

A plan emerged to match Max up with Ray, the oldest daughter, and a dinner would be arranged for them to meet. Anna had been selected to remain home to help serve and clean up, but when Max showed up, the instant he laid eyes on Anna he fell in love. And no wonder - Anna was pretty and well-built, with a "peaches and cream" complexion and jet-black hair and eyes. There was however, quite an age difference, Max being twelve years older.

Max immediately spoke to Grandpa. "Ray is nice, but I love Anna and will only marry into the family if she will be my bride." Anna cried and pleaded. She did not like Max and certainly did not feel ready for marriage - with him or with anyone. But her pleas ignored, the marriage took place.

Six months after the wedding Anna tried to leave Max and return to her parents. They refused to take her back, telling her, "It takes time to get used to living with a man; you have to get adjusted to this new way of life." And so with great sadness in her heart she returned to her husband. After all, where else could she go?

Anna quickly became disgusted with Max's sloppiness. She claimed he was not clean, and wore the same underclothes for days. He bathed only once a week, at a Coney Island Turkish bath house, a public bathing establishment. For two dollars you could even have a massage. The facility included hot and cold pools for swimming, and an extra twenty-five cents got you a large towel so you did not have to bring your own. Upon leaving, a twenty-five cent tip for the attendant was generous and proper. Max however, never gave more than ten cents.

Max preferred not to spend any money and sex must have been a problem for Anna as well! When older, I always remembered her saying, "All a man cares about is that you are good in bed, as often as he wants you to be, and you feed him good hearty meals and not spend his money!" Could that be all there was to life I wondered?

As much as Max loved Anna, she hated him. He had a wild temper and each argument sent dishes flying. At age three I can clearly recall egg yolks, spaghetti sauce, and brown gravy dripping off the kitchen wall. I never knew what they fought about, but did at times hear the words "money" and "cheating."

Whenever Anna put on make-up to go shopping, Max shouted, "Are you going to make it with the shopkeeper?" He taunted and teased her and she cried constantly. Being very sensitive, it did not take much to hurt Anna's feelings. After a while, not worth all the grief, she stopped putting on make-up and wore only wrap-around house dresses out in public.

By some bizarre miracle Anna became pregnant and a son, Morris, was born. Anna was thrilled but her joy short-lived. At the age of fourteen months the baby died of pneumonia and Anna proceeded to have a nervous breakdown. She blamed her son's death on Max and hid the baby's limp little body in a closet until she could keep her secret no longer. It took quite some time to get over this tragedy and pull herself together.

Two years later my sister Shirley was born and I arrived two years after that. Mother always said I had been a good baby, eating and sleeping like a little angel, sometimes napping for so many hours, she woke me to be sure I was still alive. When I turned three the doctor arrived with his little black bag, and Shirley and I waited on the porch until my mother's screams subsided. Being so very young, it seemed awfully difficult to understand the concept of natural childbirth, but I knew this must be a good thing, for her pain and suffering ultimately resulted in yet another addition to our little family. My brother Arthur (we called him Artie for short) entered the world.

Mark:
My name originates with Grandpa Max, and Sharon derived from Grandma Sara. We never had the opportunity to meet them and reading this is the first chance to learn about our namesakes. Sharon and I only became acquainted with one of our grandparents, Dad's mother Bertha, and only while we were young. Excursions to see her at an establishment crammed with old people had been neither pleasurable times nor did they create fond memories.

Mom's story prompted an interest in genealogy. Who are these people who preceded me? This pursuit is by far a more complicated yet enticing endeavor than expected and that journey has just begun.

Based on the 1910 New York census records, Max came to America at 39 and Sara, 35. The children ranged from age 15 to one, and Anna was 12. The archived data shows a different spelling for some of the family members, though apparently either an error in transcription or a change of name to one sounding more American, likely explains the discrepancy. Irving for example is listed as Isodore in the census, but at some point in the first few years in America, he became Irving. Anna, according to the 1930 census, married at age 18.

Sharon:
A devoted family had been unmistakably fundamental to our ancestors. In fact, the love of family represented everything – above money, jobs, and self, even though the lack of all three played a significant role in our family history and the tribulations that ensued. Perhaps my following in the family tradition had roots long before Mom and Dad met.

I followed the custom of creating a good Jewish environment, complete with children and suburban home, while Mark meandered down his own path. Extremely close as children, we grew apart and then close again for a short episode among the big trees, as you shall read. And now Mom brings Mark and I close again in the task of publishing her story.

Fun krume shidukhim kumen aroys glaykhe kinder.

From bad matches, come good children.

Max and Sara Glassberg

Anna Glassberg

Chapter Two
Life Goes On

The family hostility continued and I often believed these problems must be my fault. Through it all my father tried to keep our spirits up with singing and story-telling. He enlightened us of his childhood days in Russia. "No matter how cold outside," he would boast, "I washed my face and entire body in the snow at the rear of our house. I could take it – I am strong and will live to be a hundred and twenty years old at least - maybe even forever!" He always concluded with a hearty laugh. Shirley and I quickly learned to speak Yiddish merely from listening to his stories.

He loved to tell one "mayse" or tale in particular. One morning, he and his three cousins had to take their uncle's corpse (he had recently passed away) to the burial ground, a short walk away. Still a little dark outside, they had to climb a steep hill, and as they approached, observed two white ghosts jumping up and down. The boys became frightened, dropped the body still in its sack, and started to run. Max exclaimed, "Wait, I'll go up to the top and chase them away. I'm not afraid of any ghost!" As soon as he reached the top, the apparitions ran away. "Those weren't ghosts," laughing as he came down the hill, "they were two white sheep having a quarrel, they just looked like ghosts from a distance. They were even more frightened of me than we were of them!" I loved this story.

One Saturday morning as mother breastfed Artie, I decided to climb on her lap to be closer to them. She pushed me away so hard I went crashing down to the dining room floor as Mom yelled, "Can't you see I'm busy with the baby?" I walked away with my feelings so hurt and mother never could have imagined how this affected me.

Hating them both at the time, wishing little Artie would disappear forever so that I could be the baby again and never need to grow up.

About this time, Grandma Sara passed away and Grandpa Max remarried. I don't remember much about his new wife - except that she was fat and unfriendly, keeping mostly to herself and only associating with the children from her first marriage. Mother took Grandma's death awfully hard and came close to having another nervous breakdown, but somehow survived the ordeal.

My sister Shirley acted just like Dad - always singing, telling jokes, and having fun. Looking up to her with much admiration, I thought she was the smartest prettiest girl and I had ever seen. Truly my idol, I loved my sister so much as did everyone else. Artie, though exceptionally intelligent, was just like me, quiet and shy, and I suppose we both took after our mother.

Growing up, we were never shown any manner of affection by either parent, no hugs or kisses or even the smallest compliment to give us a lift. They remained just too wrapped up in their own troubles to notice. However, Artie was mother's pet, always served his meals first, and provided the biggest portions of the foods we all loved so much - stuffed chicken neck, chicken feet, and my favorite - the foot bones.

Life went on pretty much the same until one morning we heard a loud screeching noise in the backyard. There had been a storm the previous night and a beautiful bird had flown to a tree behind our house. Probably escaping from the local zoo during the storm, the bird comprised every color of the rainbow, and I had never seen a creature more lovely. Our neighbor tried to catch him with a broomstick and a small net but as fortune had it, the bird flew directly into our dining room through an open window! Dad went over to the window, shut it tight, and we claimed the bird as our own. We named him Rainbow.

Dad built a cage and placed it on the dining room table. My mother fed him regularly and we got a kick out of the way his tail stuck out from the side of the cage whenever he ate. It was not long before he would eat out of our hands – eggs, sunflower seeds, small nuts, and other goodies. Oh how I cherished that bird. He often perched on one of the chairs constantly creating a huge mess to clean up! None of us wanted <u>that</u> job and soon became our mother's responsibility.

We kept Rainbow for a few months until one day our mother decided to sell him to a pet shop for ten dollars, once again money taking priority over our happiness. The owner impressed with the bird, kept it outside to show him off and I enjoyed visiting Rainbow now and then. One day Rainbow escaped from his chain and flew into the nearest tree. A police officer summoned to help, fired a shot to scare the bird from its perch. His aim, however, too precise, Rainbow fell from the tree, dead the moment he hit the ground. I cried for days and blamed his demise on my mother. After all, she had been the one who sold him. A feather fallen from Rainbow's tail was my only remembrance of him. I kept it for a long time.

The Glassberg family, Mom's brothers and sisters, lived nearby – within six blocks walking distance and we had fifteen cousins, all very close to our age. We loved one another dearly and played together daily after school, on weekends, and on holidays. Everyone always visited our home since we had the only private house, yard, and plenty of room, while our relatives lived in apartment buildings.

Growing up, the only toys we owned had been roller skates and jump ropes and we spent endless hours in play. On rainy days we loved to play airport. "Plane Number Six will be landing in five minutes. All passengers please leave the plane. The next flight to Florida will be at ten o'clock tomorrow morning." I guess you could say we made our own fun.

Whenever it snowed we constructed forts and started snowball fights. Building a snowman always gave us a welcome challenge. It was remarkable that this many cousins could get along so well. I never remember any of us fighting.

Once a year, the Barnum & Bailey Circus came to town at Madison Square Garden in Manhattan. As an advertisement, elephants and caged animals of every kind paraded down our street (Blake Avenue between Howard and Graften Streets in Brooklyn). I clearly remember the elephants leaving their smelly presents in the street - always requiring a good rain and several days for the foul odor to clear! Beautiful women in bright colorful costumes marched as well. Shirley utilized crepe paper to decorate our clothing and we marched along with the parade as far as we could. We always had a ball and when the time came for our cousins to leave our house, they always ran and hid so they could stay longer.

The only doll I ever owned as a child cost five cents. It came from the corner candy store and without anyone's help I created tiny clothing. One outfit I still recall quite clearly was a black silk dress and black velvet coat with a white collar and cuffs at the sleeves trimmed with rabbit fur. Dad saved the cutting scraps from his sewing business because he knew I could always find some use for them.

At night when the house was quiet, I sat next to Dad and watched him sew. Sometimes he allowed me to help with some of the smaller jobs, such as tying the belts for the coats and dresses. I felt proud of how well I could use the sewing machine and loved the smell and feel of the fabric beneath my little fingers. To this day I cannot walk by a craft store without going in to buy something - so many colors, fabrics, and prints to choose from. This is truly paradise! I am happy to say I finally own a new modern Singer sewing machine although I can hardly do much sewing anymore because of arthritis. Everything seems to come to me a little too late. It's the story of my life.

Though capable of sewing quite well and always making my own clothing, my ability never matched Dad, the only tailor in town with the skill to weave together a hole so perfectly you could never find where it had been torn. His was a fine art. A bottle of water always sat by the ironing board, and whenever Dad pressed the garments he took a mouthful of water, sprayed it on the outfits, then pressed the clothes with a heavy cloth and steaming iron. I often wondered what his customers would think of that!

My brother Artie never came downstairs when Dad was there. He would come halfway down, sit on the stairs for a while, and then scurry back up. Although we had never been hit, Artie feared Dad's hot temper.

One Saturday night my parents had a wedding to attend and mother wanted to hire a babysitter, but Dad insisted that would be too expensive. Besides, we were getting older and they did not plan on being out late. When the time arrived for us to go to sleep, we were not prepared for the catastrophe that would transpire. The ceiling bulb had to be turned off by hand, so Shirley stood on the bed to reach it; the bulb, too tight however, would not turn. In our house when things were broken (such as the light switch) they rarely got repaired. Shirley took one of our mother's nightgowns, wrapping it around the bulb to darken the room so we could sleep.

By the time our parents came home, the end of the bed had caught fire from the sparks that had fallen from the nightgown. We were fortunate they returned in time. Lady Luck definitely shone down on us that night.

Az es brent, is a fayer.

When something's burning, there's a fire.

Chapter Three
The Lonely Years

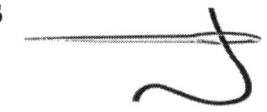

Our parents rarely went out together since Dad was always busy with another garment waiting to be finished, plus there did not seem to be a lot of spending of money. My mother never had anything nice to wear. Regardless of how much Dad worked there always seemed to be an outstanding grocery or butcher bill; and who knows what else. I was not too concerned about this but knew money problems existed.

Mother became lonely, and as quiet as she was, her need for company remained strong. Her brothers and sisters loved to play cards, and they always looked for a place to gather. Poker was their pleasure and one day my mother had an idea. "I'll run the games for them in my house," she thought.

She served lunch and kept a pot of fresh hot coffee brewing. "Hey Anna," someone would shout, "bring more hot coffee!" "I'll have one too," came another voice. They played for hours on the long dining room table and occasionally invited a few friends along. After each game, money went into a kitty for my mother's compensation. After setting aside money for food and a malted and a long salty pretzel for the children, little remained for her, but she loved the company.

My mother never played cards, but soon Grandpa Max joined in the games. If my mother got sick, the games were put on hold. They played while the children attended school and all day Saturday, Sunday, and on every holiday. Our house seemed like an active bustling adult playground, but I did not care. These times were loads of fun and a jolly good time.

Dad did not exactly approve of these card games and spent most of the time in the cellar. When he hung around it always caused arguments, and he often ate meals in the basement. Occasionally the battles became so loud and fierce that I ran into the yard and covered my ears with my hands until the incident ended.

During the card games the children loved to sit beneath the table giggling and grabbing for coins as they fell. When Grandpa Max participated, each child took turns buying him a Dixie cup filled with delicious ice cream - half vanilla and half chocolate. Because of his diabetes, this became his special treat for the day and an honor to serve him since we loved and respected him so much. Handing him his cup and little wooden spoon, I would do so with a bow. With one of his biggest smiles he returned the bow and gave a quick little wink.

On hot summer days when no poker games had been scheduled, our mother took us to Coney Island by train. Because of an immense fear of the water and those big waves, I usually stayed by the shore splashing now and then to keep cool, running like crazy as a wave approached. We brought along baskets filled with food. Hard-boiled eggs tasted especially good on the beach – crusted with sand and all. The fresh air easily brought on big appetites and we always had an abundance of fruit and plenty to drink. Perhaps the biggest delight of all, working on that great tan. Of course, Dad seldom joined us.

On rainy days we were allowed to go to the movies. For ten cents we could see two features, some cartoons, plus coming attractions. We especially loved Shirley Temple, Zorro, Betty Boop, Mickey and Minnie Mouse, and of course, Popeye and Olive. To our parents' delight, we frequently stayed to see the show twice and sometimes we would be sent with lunch to keep us away longer!

One day Dad decided to take us to the Biltmore movie theater. We were trying to complete our dish collection, one of which would be given out each week. But when we got to the ticket booth we turned around and went home. Ten cents seemed a little too much to pay for each of us. We cried and cried, but our pleas did not make a bit of difference. When it came to spending money lately, Dad had definitely turned into a "kill joy."

On Mother's Day, Dad brought home a pair of pretty purple stockings for Mom. He had found them in a garbage pail, but since they weren't ripped he thought he would take them - so proud of himself. What a miser. He told me, "When you start earning money, spending will be hard for you too." "Not true," I insisted in disbelief.

Around this time I had a boyfriend named Sol. He had tomato red hair and so many freckles that they almost concealed his face. Shirley had a boyfriend named Harry who lived around the block on Grafton Street. She would send me down to the street corner to see if he was outside so she could go look at him. I went so many times that I started to get angry, but still I did her bidding. To this day I cannot understand what she got out of simply looking at him.

Every Friday, mother cooked and cleaned all day, with the newspaper spread out on the newly washed floor to keep it clean. By day's end the paper would be completely shredded and messy. Every Jewish housewife did the same thing, and I thought to myself, how silly. We always had the same Friday night dinner - soup with fine noodles, chicken with vegetables that had been cooked in the soup, and stuffed skin from the chicken neck (sewn up with white thread). I always wanted to be sure that the thread had been taken out completely, so not to swallow it and choke. I chewed the chicken bones to bits - they were so tasty. And of course we always enjoyed potato nick (similar to a potato pancake). My mother lit five candles and said the Sabbath prayer with a napkin covering her head. The table always included two covered plates with challahs, a special Jewish braided bread used on Friday nights and for holidays. After dinner, Mom gave us each a piece of challah to nibble for mitzvah (good luck).

On special holidays, matzo balls replaced the soup noodles, and matzo replaced the challah. We referred to matzo as "hemstitched cardboard." Sometimes mother baked honey or sponge cake and the house smelled so good! After tea we enjoyed cracking nuts at the table and playing marbles with the filberts. We had such a feeling of belonging for the first time in our lives and mother tried awfully hard to keep the peace with Dad.

The Friday dinner was bought at a live chicken market. My mother picked one out and had the bird killed in a merciful manner with one clean cut by a special religious man. In this way the food would be kosher. For ten cents an elderly woman plucked the feathers and cleaned out the unnecessary insides. I loved to go along even though the market was a bloody place with a horrible smell.

Shirley had many fights with our mother, blaming Mom for her chubbiness and large breasts. Sometimes they embarrassed her so much that she threatened to cut them off. During one battle Shirley nearly jumped out the window to the yard below - though not a very high jump at any rate. Mother often chased Shirley around the dining room table, but she never got caught. Sometimes they ran around for such a long time they ended up laughing. This all seemed so silly and the table was an especially long one to run around.

Sometimes we received an ice cream pop as a special treat. I ate mine very slowly to make the delicacy last longer whereas Shirley always consumed hers fast. When she got down to the last few bites she would say, "Change with me, Clarice!" Did I do as she asked? Of course - After all, she was my sister and I figured maybe she needed this treat more than I did. I loved Shirley but at the same time felt sorry for her. This had been my method of reasoning. To me, nothing is more important than family.

Other treats we occasionally received were a colored lollipop with a ring in the middle or six caramels for five cents. I always shared the candies with Shirley and Artie - we each got two. I loved candy and still do! (To this day, if my daughter Sharon loses me at the shopping mall, she always knows where to find me - at the candy counter filling up a bag of sweet delicious treats).

I loved our house in Brooklyn with its lovely front porch and a garden with a beautiful lilac bush. When the flowers bloomed the color and aroma were magnificent. A fence of hedges surrounded the garden and I trimmed these bushes and swept the porch and walkway once a week so that mother had one less job to do. Meanwhile, Mom had to sift the ashes from the boiler stove and carry them to the curb in a barrel for pick-up. She detested this, but Dad always seemed too busy. Mom worked hard and hated her life, longing to be single again.

We had a big kitchen with a large pantry at one end of the room and a door that led out to the yard. To the left of the kitchen another door led into to a large dining room with French doors made of glass, which opened up to a huge master bedroom. The bedroom contained a full-size bed, dresser, chest, and dressing table with three moving mirrors. Standing up close to the mirrors, you could view yourself from every angle. Adjacent to the kitchen, a tiny bathroom only had a toilet seat and small sink. From the hallway, steps led down to the cellar, as well as stairs leading to the upper bedrooms which were rented out to boarders. The large upstairs bathroom had one tub that we all shared, although sometimes Dad had a live fish swimming in the water. He would hit the fish on the head with a club, scale it, and we had our dinner.

I do not recall ever brushing my teeth and never saw a dentist. When Dad had a toothache he drank a big glass of whiskey and pulled his own tooth using a pair of pliers. What guts he must have had! Ice was delivered by truck to our house and placed in a large wooden ice box and a pan kept underneath caught the water as the ice melted. A block of ice cost twenty cents and the task to empty the water twice a day became my job. In the winter we kept food in a box outside our kitchen window, which saved us money.

My mother had several nervous breakdowns, but during her well periods she went to night school and even wrote a story entitled *How to Prevent War*, which won a prize. But Dad only laughed at her and stated, "Who do you think you are, a college professor?" She became embarrassed and felt silly for thinking she could make something of herself, so she gave it up. She cried frequently and went in and out of the hospital.

Once when Mom became dreadfully sick, an aide came to our house to care for her. My mother walked from room to room, talking to herself out loud, pausing in front of the picture hanging in the dining room of Grandma and Grandpa, her parents, and speaking to them. "Dear Mom, set me free." I guess this had been her way of saying she wanted to die.

The condition of the house made me so ashamed and in the morning I made my bed as soon as I got up so that the aide would not see the tattered and torn mattress. Dad took care of us the best he could, but it was hard for him to keep up with the children and the house without Mom's full support. Our home had become so dirty and sloppy with unwashed clothes everywhere – piled on the bedroom furniture as well as on the floor. Dirty dishes sat stacked high in the sink, the house had a sour odor, and the floor felt sticky under my shoes.

During this time my Aunt Rose had promised to take me to her summer home in Sea Gate for a couple of weeks. Her house sat right on the beach in Coney Island and only the very rich could afford these homes. That part of the beach was private and even had a guard on duty twenty-four hours a day to announce incoming visitors. Shirley had also been invited, but she did not care to go. I on the other hand became so excited that I began to go through all my drawers and closet to see what I had to wear, putting a few things together - three pairs of shorts, one bathing suit, three short-sleeved shirts, and some underwear. I did not have much but didn't mind having to wash them out by hand and dry them on a hanger on the shower rod. An old worn suitcase was packed and placed under the bed to be ready to go when the call came. The summer was very hot and I literally sat by the phone waiting for Aunt Rose's call, which never came. Soon the summer ended and I knew the time had come to unpack.

Crying and wondering how she could have forgotten, I figured we must have been the black sheep of the family and she did not think our feelings mattered. "I knew this would happen," Shirley told me. "That's why I said no."

One morning not too long after this incident, I heard Dad crying in the dining room. Still very upset about what had happened with Aunt Rose, I went to see what might be wrong now. He stood in the center of the room, stark naked, holding only a pair of boxer shorts to cover his private parts as my mother taunted him, trying to pull the shorts away. She finally succeeded, calling him "an ugly pig." I always thought he was beautiful so why would she say such an insulting thing? This was the first time I had ever seen a man exposed, or cry for that matter.

I wished at that moment she was dead so I could take care of Dad and would certainly never make him cry. He pleaded, "Anna, stop this. Clarice is in the room, and this is shameful for her." Just then the aide entered the room, and taking my hand, led me outside. Hating to leave Dad alone with mother, I tried to pull away but could not. The aide, much too big and strong, gave me another shove, closing the door behind us. I hated her too.

Whenever one parent cried, I hated the other, wishing they could be on better terms. I had so much guilt, hate, and fear bottled up inside, and that's exactly where my feelings stayed for the time being, returning to haunt me later in life.

A girl named Vivian lived up the street, and although she was not very pretty, I envied her life and we became good friends. Sometimes her parents sat outside, holding hands and exchanging an occasional kiss or hug. They showered Vivian with hugs and kisses too. How I longed for that kind of love and affection. They always seemed to be talking and laughing together about one thing or another as I watched them with sadness and thought how great their lives must be. Meanwhile, my existence had become a living hell.

Vivian's family had an automobile and often took day and weekend trips. One of my favorite daydreams had been to imagine being Vivian, just for a day. For Vivian, holidays meant lots of gifts. She had beautiful dolls with long curls that said "ma—ma." Once at her house during Hanukkah, when her aunt had given her a new doll, Vivian gave me one of her older dolls to keep. She must have felt badly for me, and I became so excited that I ran right home to show her off. Shirley got envious and wanted me to share, and as we each grabbed an arm and pulled, out came both limbs - right out of their sockets. Both angry and sad for a long time, crying and eventually getting over it, then blaming myself. I should have been more willing to share the doll in the first place and Shirley really did not mean to do any harm. Besides, I loved my new doll even without arms.

Asking Dad if he might be able to fix her he responded, "What could I do?" He suggested, "Put her under the bed and pray." I did just that, but in the morning, my doll still broken, questioning Dad, he said that my prayers had not been answered. I could not understand his answer then, and still don't to this day. I guess he had little belief in God to dismiss the issue so nonchalantly.

Even today I go crazy whenever I see a doll. For my birthday, my grandchildren recently gave me a lovely doll with blond hair dressed in black velvet with a white collar and cuffs. I cried for joy at the sight of her and named the doll Vivian.

Sharon:

Mom mentions splashing at the shore, afraid to go in further. I remember going to Rockaway Beach growing up, Mom in her black one-piece bathing suit, standing at the edge, never venturing in to the waves. It is surprising that she enjoyed weekend excursions to the beach with Dad, Mark, and I. Perhaps the family time together rather than what we did is what truly mattered.

Afile der raykhster zeyger hot nit mer vi zekhtsik minut.

Even the most expensive clock has no more than sixty minutes.

Chapter Four
The Family

Time passed and Grandpa Max sold his apartment buildings, except for the one he lived in, a fifteen-minute bus ride from our house. The family started to move. Aunt Ray, Aunt Mollie, and Uncle Bernie moved into Grandpa's building and Uncle Murray now lived in Passaic, New Jersey. Uncle Arthur and Aunt Celia had bought a house near Kings Highway and Aunt Rose moved to Williamsburg. Her family was orthodox Jewish as were most people in that area. Uncle Irving, still single, performed odd jobs for a photo studio. He loved photography and ran errands, swept floors, and got lunches for everyone. He relied on tips to make a living, so when the owner closed up shop and moved to California, he longed to go, but had no money. Grandpa did not want him to go and refused to provide money for the trip.

My mother gave Uncle Irving the three hundred and fifty dollars she had saved, bought him a watch, and sent him on his way. He soon got a job on a movie set taking pictures of all the celebrities, and being quite talented quickly worked his way up to first cameraman. We were so proud to have an uncle in show business and I bragged about him to everyone.

That ended the daily card games. Occasionally the family came to visit around the holidays and out came the cards and it was fun time once again. I missed my cousins and after they left, my mother's days were once again filled with loneliness and depression. The house became much too quiet for us.

Aunt Ray and Uncle Nat had three children - Helen, Mildred, and Phil. Helen had been stricken with infant paralysis and spent her early life in and out of hospitals. She wore braces, needed crutches to walk, and someone had to be with her at all times to help her sit and stand. Despite the handicap, Helen, who was very intelligent, received an excellent education, and made her living at office jobs. For all her hardships Helen had a good social life and I do not recall ever hearing her complain. She tried to help at home as much as she could, and I watched her stand and iron clothing many times. When Uncle Nat got angry with Aunt Ray, Helen would reach up with her crutch and give him a good whack. She always had a welcoming smile on her beautiful face and was truly a very special inspirational person.

Times were difficult at our house and my mother had another breakdown, ending up in Kings County Hospital. Dad's mother, short, bent over, and very thin with dark wrinkled leather-like skin, came to take care of us and although probably not as old as she looked, she seemed to be at least one hundred. Her clothing looked like rags and she always wore the same colorless sack-like dress and sweater with a kerchief covering her thin gray hair, pulled close and tight around her face. She looked poor, and probably was based on the furniture she had in her small four-room apartment.

Sometimes we spent the night at her place, a cold flat warmed by a big black pot belly stove, wood and coal piled nearby to keep the fire burning during the long cold winter. The bathtub located in the kitchen had such high legs that I could only reach the rim by standing on a stool. A screen placed in front of the tub allowed for privacy while bathing and I somehow got the feeling she did not bathe very often.

In one corner of her kitchen sat two potato sacks filled high with peanuts. She would say, "Dig in and take as many as your hands can hold." At other times she reached in for me, but then I did not get as many, but never said anything - her shaky voice scared me a little. Nevertheless, visiting became an enjoyable experience.

Dad's mother loved to drink tea, but only drank from a glass, claiming that a cup would not keep it hot. She held her thumb at the top edge of the glass and her pointer finger at the bottom edge. That way she could drink the tea while still very hot without burning her fingers. Having tried this myself many times, to this day have not yet mastered this technique and still use a mug with a handle.

Dad's brother Moe lived at home with my grandmother. Moe played the violin and for many years studied to be a doctor but failed to pass the board exam in New York. Eventually he did become a doctor in Boston, working in a hospital clinic. I do not believe he ever married.

Sleeping three in a bed when we were growing up was not very comfortable, and Grandma made Shirley, Artie, and I sleep wearing our pull-on wool hats. Grandma said they prevented the bed bugs from crawling into our ears. Well, she didn't have to tell me twice, never putting up an argument, and wearing my hat religiously - even in hot weather! In the morning I picked all the bugs off my undershirt, throwing them on the floor, and crushing them to pieces with my shoe creating a horrible cracking sound and oozing blood – needless to say, a disgusting chore. Telling Grandma I itched all over, she just laughed. I guess this seemed funny to her and she must have been use to them.

I remained unhappy until my mother, well again, came home from the hospital. She tried her best to keep after the bed bugs and cockroaches in our house. I often got head lice and mother poured kerosene over my head and let it soak, and then washed my hair with a special soap. Once the hair dried she laid a clean white towel on the dining room table and went through the hair with a fine comb. Whenever a bug fell out she squashed it with her thumbnail, the insect snapping as blood oozed out. I felt so dirty and longed to be like other children, but it was not my mother's fault - she had been a sick dreadfully troubled woman.

Mother missed her brothers and sisters and called them often. She compared us to the other children in the family. Our cousins were always the prettiest, the smartest, and the best at everything. No wonder Shirley, Artie, and I lacked self-esteem. Dad would say to me, "Who will ever want to marry you? You're just like your mother." The interpretation of his words - I am mentally ill like Mom. Picturing myself behind bars in an institution surrounded by sick people, feeling worthless and empty inside, I was very jealous of my cousins' lives and desired so much to be like the Glassbergs.

If anyone in mother's family became sick, she dropped everything and ran over to help them, even sleeping at their apartment for a few days. She did all their cooking and cleaning, and even rinsed their bed pans while Dad took care of everything at our house, and he didn't like it one bit. "They're using you," he would tell her. "They have plenty of money and can afford to hire help." But my mother didn't care. When they beckoned, she went.

Mark:

Mom never mentioned Uncle Irving or his significance to the film industry, and she had reason to be proud, his Hollywood legacy surpassing even Mom's knowledge. He became a well-known cinematographer for Universal International Pictures, making dozens of movies in the 1940's and 1950's. His more than sixty film credits as either cameraman or cinematographer include *Cry Tough, Captain Lightfoot, The Lady Takes Flyer, Day of the Bad Man, Ride Him Cowboy, The Tarnished Angels, Bend of the River,* and *The Black Shield of Falworth,* working with big name stars such as Tony Curtis, Donald O'Connor, Eartha Kitt, Lana Turner, Chuck Connors, John Wayne, Rock Hudson, James Stewart, Robert Stack, Dorothy Malone, and the Three Stooges. Uncle Irving is perhaps best known as having discovered one of America's great actors. According to *Clint: The Life and Legend,* the official biography of Clint Eastwood, by Patrick McGilligan (1999 book by Harper Collins); Eastwood was introduced to Irving, who, impressed with how tall he appeared, introduced him to respected film director Arthur Lubin, who had worked with Irving on several films. Lubin is well-known for directing numerous Abbott and Costello movies and creating the television series about a talking horse, *Mr. Ed.*

Shpiln di griln, tantsn di vantsn.

The crickets play and the bedbugs dance.

Chapter Five
The Great Tragedy

Our lives went on as usual until November 4, 1934, when the great tragedy changed everything - the worst catastrophe to occur in my life thus far touching Shirley, now twelve, and Artie as well.

Artie was celebrating his seventh birthday party (at least he got a party. I never had one in all my ten years). All of our friends from the block were invited to the festive event. Mother had set everything up on the dining room table - plenty of candy, vanilla and chocolate ice cream Dixie cups, cake, party hats, and balloons. *Pin the tail on the donkey* dangled on one wall and gifts wrapped in colorful paper and ribbons piled high on the floor waiting to be opened. Dad was working in the cellar.

Mother hummed as she checked to be certain nothing had been forgotten to assure everything worked out perfectly for Artie's special day. During the party, Dad came up from the cellar, perhaps for lunch. An argument, the most violent yet, started in the kitchen. I remember standing in the doorway between the kitchen and dining room and mother stood directly in front of me facing Dad, waving her hands wildly in the air and screaming so loudly that I could not even make out her words, but thought perhaps it must be another one of her mental breakdowns. Dad mentioned something about money and putting two and two together, realized he must be angry about the money spent for the party. I thought to myself, he probably had not been invited anyway.

Turning his back to mother, Dad picked up a glass to get a drink from the tap. As he turned on the faucet, mother walked up behind him, and picking up a heavy glass milk bottle, hit him square on the back of the head. He let out a scream, falling to his knees holding the sink with both hands. He sobbed for a few seconds and went silent as blood ran freely from his head. I stood frozen in disbelief. How could this be happening? Should I have done something? Maybe crying out to warn Dad might have prevented this, but everything happened so fast, yet in my mind everything had been in slow motion. Assuming for sure he was dead, I shook all over, unable to move as the children came swarming in from the other room like bumble bees. One little boy exclaimed, "I will get my mother. She will call the police."

Then mother started to talk like a crazed woman. "We must run away before the police arrive. They will take out our eyes and cut out our tongues." Terrified and torn between a desire to stay with Dad and departing with her, I made the decision to save myself and ran out the door with Mom, Shirley, and Artie. We took the bus to Grandpa Max's house knowing he could determine what to do to save us. The ten-minute ride seemed to last forever and my heart thumped like it would beat out of my chest, as I hoped none of the other passengers noticed the pounding. Someone looked at me! Could they tell what had happened? I kept seeing an image of my eyes and tongue hanging on a string before me, thinking I must be going crazy too. Oh how I did not want to be blind. When we arrived my mother knocked firmly on the door. Grandpa Max soon answered, and as we stood in the hallway my mother - a bit more reserved now - told him what happened. He told us to go home. "If Max is dead," he said, "the police will take care of you." The door promptly slammed in our faces.

Thinking to myself, this can't be. How could it be possible that Grandpa – whom we loved so dearly – would not even let us in? We needed to get help, to call the police, or a hospital. Surely he should have done something. Thinking back on it now, he must have called the rest of the family after we left. Watching me shivering, he knew how frightened we had been standing in the hallway.

After what seemed like ages we went over to Aunt Ray's apartment on the top floor. My mother did not waste any time and told her that she had killed Max. Once again the door shut swiftly in her face. Next we tried Aunt Mollie and Uncle Bernie, who were on the second floor, but had the same results.

After sitting on the lobby steps for what seemed like an eternity, we went back up to Aunt Ray's place to pound on the door. This time when she opened the door my mother pushed me and Artie in before Ray realized what was happening. Then Mom turned and ran quickly down the steps with Shirley at her heels. They walked the streets well into the evening, Shirley telling me later they did not talk much and wandered aimlessly like lost souls. Since no other options existed or a place for them to go, they thought they might buy a few bottles of iodine to drink and die together in an alley. It is still difficult to believe twelve-year-old Shirley, so young and full of life, had even considered this, later admitting she had been too terrified to protest.

Fortunately my mother came to her senses later in the evening, unable to hurt her child, and took Shirley back to Uncle Bernie's. This time, as soon as he opened the door, she pushed Shirley in and ran. Fearing for Mom, Shirley tried to follow, but unable find her, Shirley went back to stay with Uncle Bernie (Mom had found a hiding place under the steps).

Back at Aunt Ray's the next morning the family talked softly in the other room. "Anna and Max must be dead. A decision will have to be made as to what will be done with the children. We could send Artie away to a sleep-over Yeshiva school." (This is a very strict religious school of higher learning for children of the Jewish faith.) Barely able to swallow the cereal placed before me, tears welled in my eyes.

We were provided money to take the bus to our school that day as well as lunch and milk money. Aunt Ray told us to go home after school and then take the bus back to her place for dinner at five o'clock. Rain pounded hard outside and we had no umbrellas...the weather matching the mood perfectly.

Horrible thoughts of being separated from my brother and sister ran through my mind. Then a silly trivial thought popped into my head - who would change ice cream pops with Shirley? Panicking and realizing it was wrong, that first night I took ten dollars from Aunt Ray's dresser. I had a plan, and intended to tell Shirley about my idea after school. We would take Artie and run far away during the night while everyone slept. It would be easy, and lying, told Shirley I had found the money, simply wanting to get out of there, with little thought as to where to go.

When we got to our house after school, Shirley cried out, "Look, here comes Dad's ghost down the street!" A white bandage wrapped around his head, as the figure came closer we knew it was Dad, alive and on his way home from the hospital. Never so happy to see anyone, joy filled my heart as we ran excitedly to meet him. I cried a river. We could stay home! As much as we loved our family, we found it hard to stay with relatives because they were always whispering and looking at us with pity in their eyes. We did not see the Glassbergs again for many years and they became strangers to us though I did think of them often.

Dad told us that our mother was still alive and then filled us in on what had happened after she left us. For a while she had walked the city streets not knowing what to do. Then she remembered her sister Rose in Williamsburg, a very religious woman who would not turn her away. She walked to the train station, her mind going wild, "What if she doesn't even let me in? Where will I go?" Before her train arrived she jumped from the elevated station platform down to the track, found an opening leading to the street far below and jumped again. Light rain started to fall as she lay unconscious, bleeding until five in the morning when a passenger on his way to work found her and called the police. They transported Mom to Kings County Hospital, placing her in a mental ward.

Her legs and ankles were broken in many places and casts had to be placed on both legs up to the thighs, with her limbs then elevated in slings. Her left ankle never healed properly and once the casts came off, although still able to walk, her left ankle remained disfigured. It was amazing she could walk at all.

Many months later Dad took us to see her. She had a soft cast on her left foot, which went from the ankle all the way up to her calf. Sitting on a porch surrounded with bars, she swayed back and forth with a blank facial expression, her hair a shaggy mess. I barely recognized my mother and recall watching her stare into space, certainly not the woman I knew and grew up with.

When finally speaking to her, asking how she felt and if she remembered me, Mom stuck out her tongue and asked if I saw the snake on it. Then she let out a crazy, demented sort of laugh as all the sick ladies nearby joined in the hysterics. Some of the women on the porch were walking around talking to themselves while others sat on the floor, half asleep. What a horrible sight to see. I was so happy to get out of there and did not see my mother again for about five years, and by then she had become well again.

Der mentsh tut hofen biz er vert antshlofen.

Man keeps hoping till he goes to his eternal slumber.

Chapter Six
The Pride of Judea

Dad took care of us the best he could, but juggling meals, laundry, housekeeping, and his job became difficult. The house still pitifully sloppy, he arranged for us to eat lunch in school each day. We were behind in our schoolwork, and homework, a big problem for me, mostly did not get done. It all became way too much for any Dad to handle alone.

One day Dad decided to speak to the principal at our school. He explained our situation and a week later a social worker arrived at our house. With her help, arrangements were made for us to be taken to a children's home called the Pride of Judea. She tried to describe what our lives would be like - no fighting, good food, clean clothes, an education, and best of all, nice people to care for us. The Pride would be as close to a normal home life as possible, and I could hardly wait to go. Just the thought of having my own bed, no bed bugs, with no need to wear a hat when sleeping, excited me to no end. Onward and upward my new life would begin. Shirley on the other hand had not been pleased at all and did not want to go. I do not know about Artie; he kept his feelings hidden.

The "home" as we called it, conducted in a semi-orthodox environment, was a private institution for children of the Jewish faith supported by the wealthy. The facility was a ten-minute ride from our house by train. We were picked up by a bus belonging to the home and joined by four other children going to another place. I kept thinking Dad would come with us, but he was not allowed on the bus, and had been in a hurry to get back down to the cellar to work. He waved to us from the door, and then went back into the house. No hugs or kisses - not that any were expected, although he could have at least said, "I'll be there soon."

As we rode away, I recall looking back at our house with tears in my eyes, sobbing softly so no one heard, whispering, "Good-bye house, I really love you." Watching until our home disappeared from sight, I assumed I would never see it again.

Happy as this had been to begin a new life, my heart also weighed heavy with fear. What will happen if we did not like our new life? Had the social worker really told us the truth, or could this be a horrible place? Finally settling down in my seat on the bus, telling myself, if it is that bad I can always run away with Shirley and Artie. I still had the ten dollars taken from Aunt Ray's dresser, saving the money in case needed someday.

The Pride of Judea building and grounds on Dumont Avenue in Brooklyn took up four square blocks. The clouds frowned and started to drizzle as we got off the bus and I thought to myself, maybe God is crying and must be feeling sad for the three of us.

About 300 children lived here at the time we arrived. Eight steps led up to the big front door, and inside, marble benches surrounded a large circular lobby. Marble plaques hung on the vast walls with the pictures and names in gold lettering of the home's primary supporters. To the left, a hallway led to the Hebrew classrooms and homework room. Mrs. Mayer, one of the teachers in charge of helping the students with homework, was short and thin, with long straight hair.

The office and library were in the lobby with a staircase leading to a tremendous yard, and another stairway went down to the clothing, sewing, and laundry rooms with hired to take care of everything. The children took meals in a large dining room with a separate room for the supervisors, while the rest of the help dined in the kitchen. The bedrooms were located upstairs with a synagogue and infirmary on the upper floor as well.

The infirmary, which reeked of disinfectant, consisted of six rooms, some with four hospital beds, and others with two. Everyone loved Doctor Demick. She had dark-skin and a pleasant accent and I loved listening to her talk. Whenever I did not feel well, Doctor Demick allowed me to stay in the infirmary for a couple of days. I started menstruating at the early age of ten and a half, and looked forward to those two days of rest especially since I hated school.

Two of the nurses, Mrs. Rosen and Mrs. Gorelic, were very kind. Freda Pearlman, who worked with them, had come to the home quite young, and Doctor Demick had taken Freda under her wing so to speak as the young girl had nowhere else to go at the time, and really wanted to become a nurse. Freda was very pretty, with jet-black hair and eyes and I loved her because she treated all the children so well. Freda worked in the infirmary until leaving to attend nursing school. She had been like one of us and I missed her very much when she left.

Getting back to our arrival at the home...it seemed as though we waited an eternity in the lobby. Eventually, Artie was taken into another room where I heard him crying. How scared he must have been without us. Then they led me into the room, but Artie was not there. What did they do with him? Seated in a chair in the center of the room, a cape draped around my shoulders, I thought to myself, "I am going to get a haircut." I wanted to ask them not to cut too short, but thought better of it and kept quiet. Then they proceeded to shave my head and suddenly realized why Artie had been crying. Where they had put him though, I dared not ask.

I began to scream, or at least thought I did. Screaming and screaming, but no sound came out. Shock overcame me, not knowing what would happen next. My clothing was taken away and pajamas were provided to wear, but I found it difficult to undress in front of strangers. Then off to the infirmary, where, thank goodness, Artie was waiting for me. Shirley joined us shortly after that, except her head was not bald. She had put up such a fight that they had not shaved her completely, although her hair had been cut much shorter. How brave she had been to fight for herself, wishing I had the guts.

Later learning that this had been done to insure no head lice, we resided in the infirmary a full week to be certain of no illnesses that might be passed on to the other children. If all this had been explained before hand, I probably would not have taken our arrival so hard. That had been about all the fear and tension this little body could handle, with any spirit left upon arrival at the home broken in those first few hours.

We were so ashamed of the way we looked. Artie wore a hat until his hair grew back; I wore a kerchief. After a week in the infirmary we were provided clothing and bedrooms upstairs.

Artie's supervisor Mrs. Braverman had her own room nearby. The older boys lived at one end of the floor, the other side for the younger ones, with the arrangement the same for girls. The bathroom, very long with white-tiled floor, included ten sinks, the same number of stalls, and one large shower with ten shower heads. Five plaid sofas, sturdy chairs, and a few lamp tables in a living room provided a place to get together and socialize. I spent a lot of time here, listening in on the conversations of the older girls, but mostly keeping to myself, and never joining in.

Meals were served family style in the dining room. Large bowls were passed around and we took as much or as little as we wished, the bowls refilled if any food ran out. Ten children were seated at each table and everyone had assigned seats within their group. Shirley, Artie, and I were unable to sit together, but we always looked around for each other to be sure we were okay. Although eating like a champ because the food tasted so good, I remained thin.

The usual traditional dinner served on Friday consisted of soup with fine noodles, chicken, vegetables, and potato nick. For holidays we had matzo. I did miss the chicken feet and stuffed skin with the white thread from home! One nice thing about the meals, we were allowed to talk at the table. On Fridays and holidays, candles were lit as a different child had a chance to pray aloud to welcome the Sabbath Queen.

We were generally happy here…it was a good home. The only work we were responsible for involved making our own beds and keeping our dresser drawers and closets clean for weekly inspection. The social worker who had come to our house had told us the truth after all.

The president, Mr. Blumberg, along with his assistant, Mrs. Schwartz, was present almost every day. She was quite beautiful, with perfectly styled hair and long nails painted bright red to match her lipstick, along with a nice slim figure and big breasts. She wore fabulous clothing, the perfect complement to her bright blond hair - a striking woman.

Mr. Blumberg and Mrs. Schwartz tried to be like a mom and dad to all the children doing whatever feasible to solve any problems that arose and to keep things running smoothly. I loved them dearly and when encountering either one of them always received either a hug or pat on the head.

All of the children came from troubled homes. Some were orphans while others had been taken away from their parents due to mental or physical abuse. One family of twelve children had a mother who jumped off the roof of an apartment building. Their father had strictly supervised visitation rights and not allowed to take any of the children out for a day because he had sexually abused one of his daughters. In another case, a mother considered dangerous had been put away in a mental institution where she remained until she died.

Rose Nadler, my supervisor and an orphan herself, had been brought to the home at a young age. As a teen she stayed on to work and eventually went to nursing school. Rose always wore the same bright red lipstick and thought it sexy to put a spot on her two front teeth. She had a boyfriend and I once asked, "What happens to the lipstick when you kiss your boyfriend?" She said I would find out one day.

The home sent me to a dentist to have my teeth checked, and considering having never learned to care for them, they were in very good shape – only one cavity. Every day clean pajamas were sent up from the laundry and placed on a bed, and always wanting to be sure to get a matching set, I waited for them and grabbed a pair for Shirley and myself. I also cleaned Shirley's drawers and closet so she passed inspection. She hated her chores and I did not want her to be punished. She didn't know how good she had it.

Ven a yosem leidt, zet kainer nit; ven er frait zich, zet di gantseh velt.

When an orphan suffers, nobody notices; when he rejoices, the whole world sees it.

The Pride of Judea

Group photo in 1935, shortly after arrival at the "home".
Mom, Shirley, and Artie are believed to be in this photograph

Chapter Seven
Dream World

I stayed in my room a lot and began to sink deeper and deeper into my own little dream world as a way of escaping the loneliness. When outdoors, I followed Shirley and her friends around. They did not seem to mind the tag along and accepted me because I was her sister. I listened quietly to all their gossip, but never spoke to them myself. Sometimes I saw Artie too.

In the morning a bell woke us promptly at seven. I showered, brushed my hair and teeth, dressed, and made my bed. Rose Nadler did not allow us to have pillows. I guess they might get wrinkled and not look good with the bed made up. Leaving the home years later it took a long time to be able to sleep on a pillow again. We made what are called hospital corners, pulling the sheet so tight that the mattress actually curled.

A short time later a second bell rang for breakfast. Hot or cold cereal, eggs, toast, juice, and milk were served. After breakfast we lined up with our groups to go to a school located outside the home. We were led by our supervisor to P.S. 202 just a few blocks away and I always walked with my head down so nobody noticed me. Some kids not from the home pointed at us and shouted, "Look, here come the orphans!" It felt like such a disgrace. Kids can be so cruel, but I did not want to be pitied either.

In class I remained lost in daydreams, rarely paying attention, but somehow making my way through each grade. I think the teachers knew I had problems. I always looked forward to the walk home because we passed a candy store. The owner stood outside holding a box of candy waiting for us to come by and each child was allowed to take one. I felt embarrassed to take a hand-out but happy to have the candy just the same. I never forgot that kind lady, blessing her in my nightly prayers saying, "Please keep the candy lady healthy and safe." Back at the home we were served milk and cake as a snack, donated from a nearby bakery and usually a delicious coffee crumb cake, and I always had two pieces. I loved to eat and never left anything on my plate - especially something sweet.

Each child took turns in the homework room and we went to a Hebrew class. The Hebrew teacher Mr. Greenfield, tall and skinny with thin lips, always dressed in a black suit. Whenever a child talked out of turn they got their hands slapped with a ruler that he carried with him, however, not a problem for me since I never spoke anyway. I liked that class, especially the Bible stories and songs. Very good at reading and writing, I always paid close attention, never daydreaming in that one class.

After classes, if not fantasizing in my room or wandering about in the yard, I spent many hours in the library reading. I loved to read, easily getting lost in a good story, often finishing an entire book in only a day or two. Mysteries were a favorite and my best grades were always for book reports.

On Saturdays after breakfast, as well as holidays, we went to the synagogue until lunchtime. I enjoyed the services and always departed with a good feeling. The Torah, covered in red velvet with gold lettering, was kept in a cabinet on a high platform. I always made sure to kiss the Torah as it made its way down the aisle.

Although Shirley did a lot of laughing on the outside, I could tell she cried on the inside. She would go up on the roof of the Pride to speak to God and make bargains with Him. "If you get me out of here by the next holiday, I promise to love you forever and be very good." I had a different approach. Instead of bribery, merely called out to Him from the rooftop to please get me home one day, hoping that if too busy, perhaps his angels might deliver my message to Him. If not, I would try again tomorrow.

So many people lived in my little fantasy world. I was collecting a harem of men including many rich and handsome actors (little did they know). Somehow I knew they were going to find me one day, though I would have to choose just one, followed by the most fantastic wedding in history with the entire world in attendance to celebrate. My gown would be the most magnificent ever created, smothered with precious jewels. Oh how I longed for that day! Could it happen? Shall I one day become the beautiful bride of my dreams? Yes... this will be real!

Believe it or not, I never fantasized about sex because all I really wanted had been someone to love me and throw their arms around me, so that I felt safe and protected. I wanted to travel the world, seeing everything out there to see.

Dad came to visit and what a surprise when he said that our mother was doing better. He visited her often although I never really asked about her because I did not care. After all, she was the reason why we were here. Shirley always got money from Dad, yelling at him until he gave her what she wanted, and then quieting down. But whenever I asked for anything he'd say, "You are not my child; you belong to your mother." I began to believe him so after a while I stopped asking for things. Artie feared him as well. He loved to draw and once asked for money to buy a set of pencils. He never got them.

I began to think my parents found me in a garbage pail. When finally leaving the Pride of Judea, I thought I needed to be very appreciative, performing errands, cleaning, and shoveling snow to show how grateful I had been to be home. I even put rollers in mother's hair every night although hated doing this. Standing behind her, I pretended to be pulling her hair out while making faces at the back of her head.

Rose Nadler left for nursing school and my new supervisor, Mrs. Cantor, was tall, skinny, and oh how mean. Someone said once she had worked in a reform school and we all hated her because she continually yelled and punished us for even the smallest of things. She wore thick pancake make-up all over her face, two round red circles of rouge on her cheeks, and pink lipstick.

One day a few girls were standing in the hallway and Mrs. Cantor wanted us all in our pajamas earlier than usual. We all moaned...but said nothing. Unafraid, Shirley called her a bitch to her face. Mrs. Cantor whacked her so hard she went sailing into a bedroom. Hurt and angry, Shirley refused to cry and when everyone applauded, the whole group got banished from going to the movies the following weekend.

Mrs. Cantor loved to play Parcheesi. When she needed a partner she walked through the halls singing, "Nice and easy - nice and easy, who will I catch to play Parcheesi?" We all ran and hid and she only caught me once. The group complained to Mrs. Schwartz and Mr. Blumberg, but all they said was how hard it is to find good help these days and we had to make the best of things, and learn to get along with her; after all, she could not be that bad could she - if they only knew.

Shirley and her friends, unafraid to raise a little hell, decided to take matters into their own hands once and for all. One evening at shower time they wet some towels with hot water, and when Mrs. Cantor opened the door to tell them their time was up, they threw the towels in her face. The hall a mess, maintenance had to be called to mop everything up. The girls were not allowed at the movies for a month but they really did not care. What mattered most, that they had gotten their revenge, though Mrs. Cantor would not leave.

Two months later one of Shirley's friends found a stray dog in the street. She put a rope around its neck and with Shirley's help, tied the dog to Mrs. Cantor's doorknob. When she opened the door she started to scream and became hysterical. "Good-bye Mrs. Cantor!" the girls yelled in unison. We finally got rid of her. The new supervisor, Mrs. Altman's ways were much more modern, calm, and understanding, always listening to our problems and trying her best to help.

The Supreme Biltmore Bluebird and other theaters in the area let the Pride of Judea's children in free on weekends to see a movie. One group went on Saturday, the other on Sunday. Only the older children went and we all had to walk in single file, which we hated but that was the safety rule.

Once a year the police and fire departments held an outing for the children from homes such as ours at Steeple Chase, a famous amusement park in Coney Island. We were given special ride tickets and a boxed lunch and allowed to roam about without supervision provided we stayed in groups of four to six. I never had the guts to ride the roller coaster, sticking to the calmer rides - the merry-go-round and the caterpillar. I always had a great time and looked forward to that time of year. I prayed for the people who made these outings possible.

Verter zol men vegn un nit tseyln.

Words should be weighed, not counted.

Chapter Eight
My First Job

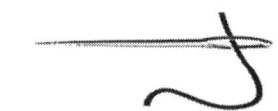

Mrs. Fleeter, the woman in charge of the younger girls in the home - mostly five and six-year-olds, was short, slim, walked with a limp, and looked Dutch, with long braided blond hair wrapping her head. I heard her complaining to Mrs. Schwartz that she needed help with her group. Mrs. Schwartz said that she could have one of the older girls assist, but had to pay them herself. I took the job for fifty cents a week and after a year she raised the pay to a dollar.

The work was hard, requiring rising early in the morning to shower, dress, and make my bed so that I could then help the young children. This was tiring but the money well worth it. The best part - not having to ask Dad for any more spending money and I could buy candy and ice pops to share with Shirley, plus a malted with a long salty pretzel for Artie. He appeared awfully thin and frail and looked like he needed them.

I helped the children get washed, dressed, and ready for breakfast, and then helped serve them while eating my breakfast at the same time. Once they were lined up, I hurried to join my group for school. I worked with ten children while Mrs. Fleeter took care of the rest. In the evening I helped the children shower, wash their heads, and get ready for bed. I kept the job for four years and then decided to give it up to concentrate more on my studies.

I was excellent at drawing and sewing but in math there were never enough fingers and toes to count on. Spelling was just as bad. I had a lot of trouble putting my thoughts into words and down on paper. If I said something in my mind it sounded perfect, but when speaking aloud, the words never came out the same. Expressing myself continued to be difficult, but determined to learn, I kept on trying. I participated in the band playing alto saxophone, but only because Shirley had joined. She played the cornet and once Shirley left the home, I gave it up. Shirley began playing music again years later after she married - the accordion, piano, and harmonica. Her teacher had always said she had a good lip for the drum - I guess because she talked so much.

During our years in the home nobody in our family came to see us except Dad. Perhaps they were ashamed of us and did not care if we were dead or alive. I often wondered if our cousins - with whom we had played with so many times, ever asked about us (and if so, what they were told). I thought about them a lot.

On weekends I stood outside by the back gate waiting for the train to pull into the station, ours the last stop on New Lots Avenue. I became so excited upon hearing the rumble on the tracks. Maybe today is the day someone would come to visit us; but it never happened. Sometimes I waited for the next train, and the next. Maybe they missed the first train and would arrive later. I always walked away with a heavy heart, and then stopped for a moment to look back to be sure I had not missed anyone. After two years I stopped watching.

When Shirley turned fourteen we were allowed to visit Dad, and on Saturdays we walked to save the car fare and keep the Sabbath. The money we saved would be spent on ice cream pops and I still changed with Shirley when mine looked bigger.

A Bar Mitzvah was going to be held for the boys who turned thirteen that year with a party in the dining room after services. Shirley received money from Dad to buy a new outfit and as usual, I got nothing, nor did I have enough money in my savings to buy anything new. A while back Dad had made me two skirts, never wearing them since I had no tops to match. The staff provided a dress from the home's clothing room to wear for the party, light blue with ugly white flowers, and much too tight. I knew then I would end up staying in my room, fantasizing that I attended the party, and having a good time. And of course, I would likely cry. Why did nothing ever work out for me? Perhaps because I was so timid and could not fight or stand up for myself.

Without my knowledge, Shirley went out and bought me two blouses using the money that Dad had given her for a dress. A peach top with two dogs embroidered on the pocket matched my blue skirt perfectly. The other blouse, made of white brushed wool with a wine scarf that wrapped around the neck, matched my wine-colored skirt. She insisted that I go to the party instead of her. I did, and actually had a good time, never forgetting what she did for me as long as I lived. Perhaps this had been her way of thanking me for cleaning her drawer and closet all those years so that she passed inspection. We helped each other out whenever we could and were as close as two sisters could be. This strong bond would last forever.

One day after about four years in the home we got a surprise. Mrs. Schwartz called my sister, brother, and I into the library room, and when we arrived, were startled to see Grandpa Max and Uncle Irving. Our uncle had come to visit from California, and although he had been in New York many times before, this was his first visit to see us. How very handsome he looked! We stood before him with our heads down because we felt shy, ashamed, and had nothing to say. Even Shirley, never at a loss for words, stood silent. They stayed only a few minutes, then left saying, "We'll be back tomorrow to spend more time getting to know each other." They apologized for not preparing us ahead of time for their visit but never did come back. It really did not bother us, but when we finally went home, mother insisted that we keep in touch with them since they were her family. In spite of everything Mom had put us through; we were good children and could never hurt her feelings.

Besides building my own little dream world, I had created a wall around myself so nothing could hurt me. I wanted to become stronger, yet at the same time did not want to lose the ability to forgive. I guess because I needed so badly to be loved, I could never get mad or say no to anyone; otherwise I might lose their respect. I assumed that by doing whatever possible for people - no matter how hard this might be, they would care about me and like me. What a fool! When depressed, I picked myself right back up and tried to start over again. It became the only way to survive.

After five years at the Pride of Judea, Shirley received permission to visit Dad for the summer, returning two weeks before the start of school in September. Meanwhile, the home sent me to Camp Vacamas in the Adirondacks for two weeks, which I hated. The children were all strangers to me and I felt so alone. I never went swimming, but sat and watched the others splashing around and having fun; the longest two weeks of my life, and consequently the following summer, refused to go. Shirley, on the other hand, did not want to come back to the Pride.

Dad agreed to let Shirley stay at the house and I missed her terribly. My mother had come back home and literally took over the house, leaving Dad to sleep in the cellar on the cutting table. At least she had been nice enough to give him a pillow and blanket. He wanted to start a new life with her, but she would not hear of it. In fact, I was amazed that he was not afraid of her.

Mother came to visit Artie and me every weekend bringing the best Ebinger cakes for Artie, taking him down to the dining room and letting him eat as much as he wanted, calling me down for the leftovers. Knowing he was her favorite, it was best to remain silent. Maybe I did not really belong to her either, often wondering who I was and where I came from.

Aside from my job helping the younger children, lots of time involved helping the girls finish their graduation dresses. Everyone had to be in uniform and Mrs. Schwartz assisted me with the sewing. I really desired to take a nursing course, but was not allowed. Instead, Mrs. Schwartz made me take sewing and art courses at Girls' Commercial High School. I guess she figured I could not handle the nursing course; sewing and art did come easy to me.

I went home to live with my parents after six years, and Artie six months after that. Glad to be with Shirley again, at first feared my mother, than soon realized that she was well again and did not intend to hurt us. I was sixteen years old when I left the Pride of Judea.

Mark:
Sitting and typing with a few tears slowly making their way down my check, oh how I wish what seems like a lifetime ago, I knew Mom's story. The lesson learned years too late is simple. Instead of fighting with your parents when you are growing up, take the opportunity to learn who they are. Perhaps there is a reason they know more than you. Life's wisdom comes from experiences that only time can create.

Sharon:
Ebinger, a New York bakery established in the late 1800's producing very rich cakes and pies, went bankrupt in 1972. Camp Vacamas has been providing summer camp experiences for children in need since 1924.

When our Aunt Shirley first left the Pride of Judea, she worked several jobs to raise money to prove that their father could make a safe home for the children. Then Mom joined Shirley in earning money to bring their brother Artie home.

Di tsayt iz tayerer fun gelt.

Time is more precious than money.

Artie with parents Max and Anna

Shirley

Mom

Chapter Nine
Life At Home

The upstairs bedrooms were still rented to boarders, so I cleaned the rooms, changed the linens, dusted, and washed the floors. The tenants rarely made an appearance, but they left a dollar tip on the dresser. What a delight to earn spending money. My mother decided to get a job and wanted to start a small shop at home selling stockings and underwear, and asked her brothers and sisters to loan her money. After talking it over they said they were sorry, but had "reached the bottom of the barrel" in the support they could provide. I do not know how they came up with that. Mom had been away for five years and neither she nor her three children at the Pride of Judea had received any help from them during this period.

So Mom went door to door with a heavy suitcase containing samples from which she could take orders. She traveled by train to Delancey Street on the east side of Manhattan to pick up her products, a difficult task with her bad feet. Her shoes, made special by an orthopedic store at a cost of one hundred dollars, went all the way up to her knees. Mom's work provided a small income, but sometimes upon delivery the customer changed his mind, and that meant an extra trip into the city to return the merchandise.

Shirley soon got a job too, and I quit high school during my last year to do the same. But there were periods when none of us had employment and Dad could not give us much money; his dressmaking business doing poorly during those times, finances really got tight. Shirley would go to Dad to ask for help to buy food, but with tears in his eyes he would say, "I'm starving too."

One day Shirley noticed something cooking on the stove in a pot that Dad normally used for heating the irons. She asked him to share the chicken soup with his children, but still angry because

Mom refused to take him back, he merely replied, "No, if I do your mother will eat it all." Shirley yelled at him until he got so mad that he spilled the entire pot of soup on the floor. "Here it is," he shouted stomping all over it, "now no one will eat." My mother told him to get out, but he refused to leave. She called her brother Bernie, who came to the house that afternoon and somehow managed to half push, half carry a ranting and raving Dad out to the street. He stayed with his mother for a while and eventually found himself a small three-room apartment a few blocks away. Artie, Shirley, and I visited him often, cleaning his apartment, and stealing some food at the same time. A piece of bread here, an egg or cracker there - whatever we could get our hands on and fit in our pockets.

Around this time a telephone call came from Selma Levitt, one of the girls from my group at the Pride of Judea. She had left six months before I did and wanted me to come to her sweet sixteen party. The occasion chaperoned by her parents, would be my very first social event outside of the Pride of Judea. Although scared and wondering how to act and what to talk about, decided to go just the same, telling myself I have to start somewhere.

The party included a small group of boys and girls with plenty to eat and drink and decorations with bright balloons and streamers. We played a few standard party games...and then came the one I dreaded - Spin the Bottle. Trying to hide in a corner and not look conspicuous, one boy noticed and I had to go into the next room to kiss him. Turning to give him a cheek, he quickly pulled my face around to his for a juicy smack on the lips - my first kiss. I became red-faced and angry, slapped his face, and stormed out of the room. After the party, Selma's mother asked me what had happened. When I told her she just laughed. "From the way you acted, I thought he had done something awful," she chuckled. I was so embarrassed!

A few days later Selma came by with her fiancé and they took Shirley and me for a ride in their rumble seat car. It started to rain, and although they rushed to get us home, we got soaked. I never saw her again after that, but heard she moved out of state.

After the party incident, Shirley tried to help me out of my shell, taking me along to listen and learn when she had a date. Her boyfriends weren't exactly thrilled with little sister tagging along, but they had no choice. The boys really liked Shirley, enjoyed her company, and she refused to go otherwise. Following them did not help me much because I still lived deep inside my own little fantasy world, dancing with Gene Kelly or Fred Astaire, or planning my dream wedding.

Occasionally if I happened to be set up on a date, Shirley wrote out a mock conversation for me to study and memorize. It never worked out because the guy never said anything that she had written for his part, and that just left me sounding confused and ridiculous. In my mind I tried thinking ahead to what to say next, wishing sometimes the ground would open and swallow me up. Life became miserable and most nights involved crying myself to sleep, wanting to be a real person and to live my fantasies, not just imagine them. My mother had always told me, "If the first part of your life is bad, as the world turns the rest of your life becomes good." Today at seventy-one, the second part still hasn't arrived.

Dad liked to say, "The world is a playground. We were put on earth to play; you just have to know how to do it." Shirley liked his words best because she knew how to master the art of having fun. Because financially times were getting so bad, all of our clothing was given to us by neighbors when the seasons changed. This meant that in the winter, we were given their old summer things and in the summer, we were wearing heavy winter garments. Sometimes they were in very good condition; nevertheless, we were always in the wrong season and we saved our good clothes for dates.

When Grandpa Max died he left his house to Uncle Bernie, the money to be shared with the entire family should the house bring a profit or be sold. However, with no written will, everything had been done on blind faith because Grandpa presumed Uncle Bernie, a lawyer, could be trusted. No one got anything. The relatives thought about taking him to court, but never did. They were proud people and did not want to bring disgrace upon the family.

During World War II, if mother needed monetary help, she received sugar ration stamps. She also traded in her jewelry for food and other necessities hoping to be able to pay off her debts and get her possessions back some day, though never did.

Uncle Irving, now married to a lovely lady, came to New York for a visit. His beautiful wife was slim with short blond hair and had nails that were painted a bright red. Whenever she put on her silk stockings she wore little white gloves. Warm, friendly, and pretty, I thought she was the cat's meow. They stayed with Aunt Ray for two weeks, and before they left, Ray had a dinner party for them. Mother, Shirley, Artie, and I however, were not invited, having been told that they simply did have not enough room around the table. The truth - they knew we did not possess enough money to help chip in for the food. My mother said her good-byes by telephone. To this day, I still feel sad that she did not get to give Uncle Irving a hug or kiss. That turned out to be the last time she ever saw her brother.

Ver shemt zich fun zeineh mishpocheh, oif dem iz kain brocheh.

Whoever is ashamed of his family will have no blessings.

Chapter Ten
From a House to a Shoe Box

One sunny afternoon not too long after Uncle Irving's visit, my mother took us to a nearby park. The bees were buzzing, the flowers were blooming, and people were everywhere. We were tossing a big blue beach ball back and forth having a grand old time (it didn't take much to make us happy). We stayed for two hours and then began our walk home, unprepared for what awaited us - our house in flames, the neighbors gathered outside as the firemen on the scene with their big red trucks busily hosed down what remained of our home. Considerably damaged, though not beyond repair, by the time the trucks left everything was soaking wet and the smell of burnt chicken feathers (from our bedding) lingered in the air.

Because we did not have enough insurance, the bank wanted our mortgage paid up. We did not have enough money for the repairs, but the bank said they could wait if the damage could be fixed. If the rest of the Glassberg family had been willing to pitch in, it meant just a little from each one. But they refused and Dad did not have any money either. Mother called Uncle Irving who sent a check for three hundred and fifty dollars - the amount mother had loaned him to go to California. Not nearly enough, things were looking bad, and we had to be out of the house in a few months with nowhere to go.

Our home would be auctioned off for the price of the mortgage to a family who could afford to make the repairs. Luckily my mother found an apartment a short distance away on Bristol Street near Pitkin Avenue on the very day we were to be evicted. The building was a four-story walk-up; we were on the second floor. A railroad flat containing four rooms, walking in through the front door you could see straight through the apartment to the last bedroom. After living in a house it felt like moving into a shoe box. When I sat on the toilet it shook from side to side, and of course it was never repaired. Life was not being fair and we cried together often.

Dad had a heart attack and had to retire. He had asthma and coughed constantly but still smoked three packs of cigarettes a day. Sometimes Dad bought loose tobacco and paper and rolled his own cigarettes using a small machine, smoking every cigarette until the tip, wet and brown, burned his fingers. Shirley and I began to smoke and in those days one cigarette cost a penny. I started with five a day, soon increasing to a pack, while Shirley smoked nearly two packs a day. I thought it so sexy to blow the smoke out of my nose, and if possible would have blown it out of my eyes and ears as well. Oh, how I loved to smoke. Artie never took up the habit, spending most of his free time building model boats and planes, flying the aircraft by remote control at a wide open field on Long Island where many other boys launched their planes. Occasionally he did have a crash or two. Thank goodness he was not a real pilot.

Alts iz nit puter vos kumt aroys fun der ku.

All is not butter that comes from a cow.

Chapter Eleven
Making New Friends

After living in our shoe box for a short time I made friends with a couple of girls who lived three houses down from us - Roslyn and Estelle. Roslyn had a boyfriend named Bernie who had already been married and divorced. He promised to marry her someday but always managed to come up with one excuse or another so I doubt it ever happened. Roslyn soon moved away and we kept in touch by phone for a while. Then she moved again, and that was the last I heard of her.

Estelle went with a nice guy named Issie for about a year, then they married, moved to the Bronx, and had twins - a boy and a girl. Two years later they bought a mobile home in Miami, Florida and had their third child. Although we kept in touch by mail and phone we had not seen one another for many years. (In 1994 she came to New York for a visit after Issie had died of a stroke. It was so nice to see her again and to reminisce about our teen years. Shortly after she returned home, she called to tell me she had been diagnosed with brain cancer, determined to beat the disease, but died very quickly after that. I am so glad I had the chance to see her one last time.)

Shirley and I decided to take a job in a toy factory making miniature plastic doll furniture. We worked at a table with a girl named Florence Tilchen and soon became good friends. Flo as we called her, knew I did not talk much but liked me just the same. It was clean work, only a short bus ride from where we lived, and decent pay.

Flo, very pretty, with jet-black hair and a beautiful face and figure was like Shirley, full of fun and capable of talking up a storm. The boys flocked to her like moths to a flame, and I suppose Flo felt sorry for me and tried to provide advice on dating. Flo, a terrific dancer, loved to attend dances, meeting the boys she later dated. Sometimes I accompanied her but always ended up a wallflower. Still dreadful at making conversation, on rare occasions when asked to dance, the boy never did stay to talk. These were late nights and I often slept over Flo's apartment. Her brother Sam, also single, always said hello and good-bye and acted generally very nice and polite to me. I did not realize it at the time, but he too was very shy and not much of a talker. Flo and I used the bedroom, her mom slept in the living room, and Sam slept on a cot in the kitchen.

The toy business had slowed and after about a year we were all out of work. I found another job at the Brooklyn Jewish Hospital in their clinic, a twenty-minute ride from our home by trolley car. Each day would be set up for a different type of examination, and I loved "baby day" the best. I weighed and measured each baby and sterilized the instruments to get them ready for the doctor. I earned sixteen dollars a week plus free lunch in the dining room.

During World War II everyone went to work in the defense plants so Shirley and I secured jobs making small parts for planes and ships. I worked on an assembly line doing easy work for good pay. Flo did not join us but we still kept in touch and her brother Sam had been stationed in the army, overseas in England. Shirley worked in a screened room caged like a monkey. She went busily about her work babbling along like always, and somehow talked her manager into a date.

Nat Gelfand, very handsome and boyish-looking, was a year older than Shirley and both friendly and a bit shy at the same time. He came from a family of fifteen children and his father had passed away a few years earlier. Shirley and Nat got along great, always keeping one another laughing. He loved her personality, and she in turn brought out the best in him. Nat smoked as well so whenever he came to visit a cloud of smoke always hovered over the rooms. They dated for a few months and then became engaged. Her diamond ring was magnificent. Shirley loved diamonds more than anything and we nicknamed her "Diamond Lil."

They had wanted a small wedding but our mother insisted on a big affair, but with the war now over we were out of work and had no money. My mother told Shirley to ask Dad to pay for the wedding. Shirley could care less whether he gave her money or not because she did not want anything elaborate, but she asked and to everyone's surprise, he agreed.

The night before the wedding Nat came to see Shirley. Her hair set in rollers and covered with a kerchief, when he went to kiss her she blew a huge bubble out of her mouth that nearly covered his face. She loved chewing bubble gum - and surprising people! They had a wonderful wedding with Shirley dressed in a gown with a long train of white satin, lace, and beads plus a fingertip veil attached to a feather cap. A three-piece band kept everyone dancing while the walls literally shook. As maid of honor in a light blue gown, I played the part of the princess from my dreams.

The entire Glassberg family attended the wedding although Shirley preferred not to invite them, but mother insisted. While very happy for my sister, in some ways wished it had been me. But why would anyone want someone so quiet and shy, an unattractive "plain Jane" with no personality, not much fun, and lacking intelligence? With no self-esteem, this is how I saw myself, and the image seemed accurate. And yet I remained perfect….within my fantasies.

The newlyweds went to the Nevele Hotel in the Catskills, a popular honeymoon spot at the time. After a week they came home and moved into Nat's brother's house where they shared a small bedroom on the upper floor. And of course, Shirley became unhappy. She cooked on a small one-burner stove – like the style Dad had used to heat his irons, and dishes and pots were washed in the bathroom in a tiny sink. Nat tried to be a huge help, but it was still hard to live this way. They resided here a few months when a small fire broke out in the bedroom, so they came to live with us in the shoebox apartment until they could find a place of their own. Despite the crowded conditions we all had lots of fun together.

A lustiger dales gait iber alles.

Happy poverty overcomes everything.

Chapter Twelve
Nightmares and Visions

Nat and Shirley were up to smoking three packs a day though I got by on one. Whenever we put out the cigarettes in the ashtray we were always careful not to break them so that if we ran short at night we could share the burns. A disgusting habit I know, but we were hooked, always a haze of smoke lingering in the house that my mother and Artie detested. "We're living and breathing in a nicotine cloud of smoke," Artie constantly complained, and he was right. Even when we removed our nail polish, our nails were stained yellow.

Shirley became pregnant and several strange events followed. She had a nightmare that frightened her to death, dreaming of giving birth to a beautiful blond eight-and-a-half pound baby girl. While taking the infant for a walk in a carriage decorated with bright pink bows, a woman passing by looked in to admire her. As the baby turned her way however, the infant had the face of a wrinkled old lady. Shirley immediately fled to her doctor for an examination, but with only two months to go, he assured her that everything would be fine.

Time flew and before we knew it Shirley went into labor. We did not have a car so Nat called for a taxi, but on the way down the stairs her water broke. We wrapped her in big towels and Nat promised to call home as soon as the baby arrived. Wanting to be awake when the phone call came, at about one o'clock in the morning, Mom, Artie, and I set a pot of coffee to brew. Before it had finished perking, mother fell asleep on the couch, waking with a start a short time later, jumping up and exclaiming, "Something is wrong with the baby!" In a dream, a white dove glided down from the sky, placed the baby on the ground, and then flew away. Then the dove quickly returned, scooping up the baby and flying away.

"That's a bad omen," said my superstitious mother, always telling us to "knock on wood" and "bite your tongues when you see a funeral pass by." I on the other hand did not believe such things for a minute.

By six in the morning we were on our second pot of coffee and snacking on chocolate cake when the phone rang. It was Nat. Shirley had indeed delivered a blond eight-pound baby girl, but had trouble breathing and a respirator did not help. Numerous doctors were called in but none could figure out the problem. Her lungs were fine as were all the vital signs. Shirley wanted to see the baby, but thought this might make the situation that much harder for her if the baby failed to survive. She and Nat both cried bitter tears as they waited with hope and prayer.

The next morning the woman in the bed across from Shirley had her baby, and pretty flowers sat on the table next to the bed. But as Shirley stared at them, the bouquet transformed into the image of a woman with a soft glowing face and shawl covered head holding a baby in her arms. Shirley blinked a few times to be sure the image was not a dream. Then the woman held the baby out to Shirley, but as she lifted her arms to take the child the baby disappeared. Shirley tried hard to regain the vision, but it had vanished. Had this merely been her imagination or a premonition? A few minutes later the answer came - Shirley's doctor informed her that the baby had died.

An autopsy revealed that the adrenal glands behind the baby's kidneys had been bleeding, likely during the birth, and in those days no medical help existed for this condition. Nat took care of the burial although Shirley preferred they had given the baby a name and planned a funeral. She had after all lived for almost two days. Shirley had hoped to have a grave to visit at least once a year, leaving a stone as is customary in the Jewish religion. I recently found out that the infant's remains had gone to Potter's Field. For a long time Shirley feared having another baby.

Nat and Shirley got an apartment on Sheffield Avenue in Brooklyn, a meager four room quarters next to the fire department - very noisy. Our father feared being alone so he constantly cried to

Shirley until she felt so bad she decided to let him live with them. Nat was out of work and Dad offered to go into a cleaning store business with him. Dad assumed they could make a go of it working together and at first they had plenty of customers, but with the store in a very poor part of town, people began paying for their cleaning services with cheap costume jewelry and within a year they were out of business. Nat then got a job managing a raincoat factory and things were looking up.

Shirley took good care of Dad even though he gave her such a hard time with comments such as, "If you were lying on the floor desperate for a drink of water, I'd step over you and walk away". Whenever she went out he told her," I am sure you will find me dead when you get home." Finally Shirley could take it no longer and found him a pleasant furnished room nearby and brought him meals even though he did not deserve it. Any other daughter would have disowned him.

I found another job in a factory, this time making plastic garment bags on a sewing machine. It was piece work, meaning that pay was provided according to how much product had been produced. In order for the plastic to slide through the feeder easily, it had to be kept heavily oiled, which stained my clothes. The work was dirty, but being very fast earned me between fifty and sixty dollars a week (other girls were earning only thirty-five). On pay days I handed my mother the closed cash pay envelope and she gave me as much spending money as she could. At least with this help, physically unable to do it any longer, Mom gave up the door-to-door sales.

Shirley became pregnant again, calling our mother on the phone every day, and during one such call Mom suddenly stopped talking and began making strange sounds. Shirley immediately sent Nat to check on her since Artie and I were not home at the time. Nat had to climb up the fire escape and through a window, finding her not moving, and still clutching the phone. Her doctor was summoned and his diagnosis - a massive stroke. He advised us to get her to a hospital immediately, otherwise she was unlikely to last more than a day, but Shirley wanted her home. We hardly had a mother all these years since she had spent so much time in hospitals and Shirley suspected that Mom would be better off with us - nothing could beat the loving care of one's family. Artie and I agreed knowing it would be difficult, but we respected Shirley's opinion.

We rented a hospital bed and hired a nurse's aide. Nat and Shirley closed up their apartment temporarily and moved in with us, pooling our meager savings to help make ends meet. Artie and Nat kept their outside jobs while Shirley and I stayed home to help the aide.

My mother was paralyzed from the neck down, unable to move or speak. The aide managed to get some fluids into her and after three days Mom began to move her hands. We gave her a pot and spoon to bang on when she needed something, after which we had to figure out what she wanted. In a few days she graduated to pencil and paper. At first we could barely make out her scribbling, but we were just so happy with the improvement and eventually she could squeeze out a few words.

Shirley used torn-up linens as diapers while Nat helped mother move her bowels using a rubber glove. He had been a medic in the army and so wonderful of him to do this. I could never thank him enough and told him that if his family ever needed my help, I would always be there for them. A promise later honored many times. Of course, Nat did it more for Shirley's sake because he loved her so deeply.

The doctor, amazed at her improvement told us, "She must have physical therapy now, to get her walking". But to afford that, our savings now almost gone, we had to let the aide go. Mother's therapist came twice a week but after a short time we could no longer afford to continue to pay her. Shirley and I tried to help her exercise, removing her from the bed and trying to walk her around the room, but when we were finished, we could never get her back into bed, lying her down on the floor until the men came home from work. With no other options, we agreed to put her into a hospital for rehabilitation.

Meanwhile, Dad had another heart attack and had fallen in the street. He arrived at the hospital in bad shape and now we found ourselves going back and forth to the hospital visiting both parents. After weeks of hospital therapy we were told that our mother's legs were permanently damaged - confined to a wheelchair, never to walk again. She became deeply depressed, refusing to eat, drink, or take medication - mother no longer wanted to live. The small blood vessels in her head began to break and doctors transferred her to the medical ward in Kings County Hospital.

Shirley and Nat went back to their own place to live and I returned to my job. After work each evening, Shirley and I met Artie at the hospital, although Shirley could not go up to Mom's room due to a phobic fear of death, staying in the lobby at least helped her to feel close. Frail and yellow with fever blisters covering her barely recognizable face, mother slipped into a coma.

Dad passed away in the hospital at age sixty-six. No feelings existed one way or the other, and at the funeral services I only pretended to cry. He had an open coffin and looked very handsome – as if merely in a deep sleep. Pleased to have Dad out of my life sounds cold and cruel, but I was happy not to have to visit him anymore. Dad had planned to live to be at least one hundred and twenty – it was not meant to be.

Mother died a few months later at the age of fifty-four with Artie at her side when she took her last breath. Because she had looked so terrible at the end, her coffin remained closed. I pretended to cry for her, thinking to myself, how terrible a person I must be not to care, but I was just so tired of it all.

From Ellen (Artie's daughter):

My dad didn't talk much about living in the home (Pride of Judea). He never came to terms with it. It was at Aunt Clarice's funeral that he told me about their dad's funeral. He was standing at the edge of the grave and crying and someone asked him why….after all Max had not been a very good father.

Dad said he was not crying for what he lost, but for what he never had. This was one of the very few revealing moments of his deep emotions about his childhood.

Di velt iz sheyn nor di mentshn makhn zi mies.

The world is beautiful but people make it ugly.

Artie's love of photography and art followed him through life

Chapter Thirteen
Nat's Tales

Artie and I stayed on at the "shoe box" apartment while Shirley and Nat went on with their own lives. Shirley became very close with many of Nat's brothers and sisters and whenever they got together, told stories of how life had been at their house when they were young. After all, there were fifteen of them! The older children helped with the care of the little ones. Nat's mother placed some of the babies to sleep in dresser drawers, lining each with soft blankets to ensure each child was provided warmth and comfort. What a sight this must have been! It's too bad they didn't take pictures.

When the older children came in for lunch, a long salami would be hung from the kitchen ceiling on a rope. Each child chopped off a portion, tore off a piece of bread from the large loaf on the table, dipped the meat into a jar of mustard, and proceeded to eat. Sometimes they had a huge pot of vegetable soup, each child filling their own bowl with a ladle, tearing off a chunk of bread for dipping - a healthy meal with plenty for seconds.

When they were babies, ketchup bottles with nipples were used to serve milk, lined up on the table, each child strolled down the line until he or she found his own nipple. Somehow they always knew. Years later, it would be the same with the bubble gum stuck under the table during meals. After dinner, when they wanted to resume chewing, each child always knew his or her own piece.

Once a year the family went to the cemetery to visit their father's grave, opening a bridge table or two and sitting on folding chairs, they stayed for a few hours. They ate lunch, drank wine, and played cards to keep their dad's spirit company. They babbled on and on, telling jokes and laughing and having a grand old time. "Come on dad," someone would say, "let's see your cards!"

Nat's mother began looking for a larger apartment for the family and found one on the top floor of a private home. She did not happen to mention the number of children she had to the landlady, moving in at night very quietly. The next morning his mother happened to sleep late, and when she awoke, the fifteen children were already outside playing in the yard with a bunch of other kids. They were making plenty of noise and Nat's mother heard the landlady coming up the stairs. Nat's mother apologized for the racket. "Don't worry," said the landlady, "the other twelve children are mine!" They lived there for a long time.

Shirley gave birth to another eight-pound baby girl named Arlene. Although generally healthy, she was quite colic and cried constantly. Sucking her thumb did not provide much relief, but it must have made her happy in some way, because she kept the habit until she got married. Shirley tried giving her new foods and different types of milk, but nothing seemed to help. The doctor said she would grow out of the digestion issue, and she did - at the age of five. I hardly ever saw Arlene without tears running down her little cheeks, into her mouth and down her neck, just like Niagara Falls.

When Arlene turned a year old she wanted badly to walk. That made her content. So whoever (often me) had some free time walked her around, holding her hand in and out of the house. This went on for hours at a time and it seemed my legs always gave out after a while, but hers never did. I did this for Shirley; she deserved an occasional rest. When Arlene finally went down for a nap, we all breathed a sigh of relief, hoping it would be a quiet and long peaceful sleep.

At night Arlene cried a lot too, and the neighbors hollered, "Give that baby a bottle!" Little did they know she was on her third one. First came the milk, then the juice, followed by water and tea - a nightly routine.

I went over to Shirley's every night after work to help, often buying clothes for Arlene with my pay. I did not mind spending money on her; she was just SO cute. I loved her - after all, this was Shirley's child.

One day we received a telephone call from my friend Flo Tilchen, who I had not seen since Shirley's wedding. She had married a guy named Jerry Gilbert, who had a poor heart with no surgery available for his condition, but Flo stuck by him and somehow felt sure he would be well. I paid her a visit and we spent a very enjoyable afternoon reminiscing about our dating days.

We attended a dance in Coney Island where I met Leonard Farin, the Tyrone Power type often lingering in my dreams and fantasies. He had dark skin and black hair and we dated many times. If he had asked I surely would have married him. On one particular date we were having a drink together at the bar and I asked him his opinion of me - big mistake. He laughed, "You're stupid and boring." I was sorry to have inquired, but deep down knew he was right. Next the topic of sex came up. He saw nothing wrong with it as long as you cared for the person. My response, "As long as you're married the sky's the limit." And that was the last time I ever saw Leonard Farin.

Flo's husband Jerry was tall and good-looking with curly blond hair, which compared to Flo's dark hair made quite a contrast. They looked great together and he became a very good husband and father (they later had a daughter, another Arlene).

Flo told me her brother Sam had been asking about me and wanted to set up a date. I was so excited! I remembered him with his nice build, and just a little taller than me, a nice conservative dresser and very handsome. Somehow I just knew this had to work out, after all, they weren't lined up at the door!

Sam arrived at Shirley's house one Saturday at seven in the evening. Shirley liked him immediately and felt he was just my type - shy and reserved. As we walked down the front steps I tripped and fell. Sam always said I fell for him on our first date. Conversation remained very strained, trying hard to squeeze out sentences without my mind going blank. However, Sam did not seem to mind the silence. I guess he really liked me. We were at the beach on one occasion and I could not take my eyes off another couple sitting nearby as they talked and laughed together continuously. What did they find to talk about for four hours? I wished to have heard that conversation! Trying to put thoughts into words, they always came out all wrong. I tried my best to think ahead but that did not work either.

Six months after our first date Sam purchased a beautiful gold watch with five stones on each side - we were engaged. I was twenty-seven and he thirty-seven. He wanted to wait until his three sisters got married before we got hitched since he provided the sole support of their household. The time flew.

Marbe dvorim, marbe shtus — vos vintsiker m'ret, gezinter iz.

A lot of words, a lot of foolishness — the less you talk, the healthier.

Chapter Fourteen
A Voice from the Grave

Sam bought a wedding band that matched the watch, white gold surrounded by ten stones. We were ready to marry and Sam's mother planned a small house party and agreed to do all the cooking and baking. "I'll have open house all day and we'll invite the neighbors," she said. We had no money for anything else and I was heartbroken. There would be no gown, no music, no flowers - only a Rabbi and a quick ceremony. I cried and cried, but to no avail. The dream wedding I waited for all my life would never be real.

Sam and I started a bank account and I kept the book. He gave me ten dollars a week to deposit but I don't think he trusted me, so before long he took the book away. "I will take care of it myself," he said. He had given one of his sisters a bank account when she was single and every time he put money in, she took cash out and spent it, so I assume he figured I would do the same.

At times wanting to call off our wedding, but Dad's words rang in my ears, "Who will ever marry you?" Sam would make a presentable husband so I held on for dear life. Sam knew he had to wait for sex until after we were married and I was partly at fault here, due to the fact that I could not to talk about these things with him.

Sometimes disagreeing with Sam, but preferring to avoid a fight, stayed inside a "shell" and kept my mouth shut. Sam became angry because I did not want to live with his mother, Bertha. He did not want her to have to live alone, and knew we could save some money by staying in her apartment. Having taken care of my mother for many years, the time had come to be on my own, and I stood firm in this decision. Sam had three sisters and I insisted they could take responsibility for Bertha, but agreed to contribute twenty dollars a week to her support. Eventually Bertha decided to share her apartment with her life-long friend Rachel. The arrangement lasted barely six months as they fought constantly. Bertha felt cold and wanted the windows shut; Rachel was hot. Rachel felt they needed a new floor and Bertha did not want to have to ask Sam for money. Every argument seemed to be over something petty and Rachel soon moved out.

My sister Shirley started having some mental problems and went under the care of a psychologist, Dr. Martin Agan. She told me all about her sessions and I realized I needed to go too, but feared Sam might find out. I had never really told him the truth about my life. He knew about the orphanage, but thought we were sent there because my mother had been in a car accident. "Dad couldn't take care of us," I had told him, "so we stayed at the home until she got better." He never asked how long we lived there so I never told him.

One Tuesday after work, Artie and I had dinner at Shirley's house. On the bus ride home I kept hearing a voice inside my head, "After Artie goes to sleep," it said, "sit in the kitchen and wait for me." The voice was not recognizable…and wait for whom I wondered? No answer came, and I fought hard to remain calm. Don't panic I thought to myself.

Artie went to sleep around ten-thirty as I sat in the kitchen sipping tea and waited. Around two o'clock it happened, my mother, calling from the grave, loud and clear. "Clarice, open the window and let me in. I must speak to you." I didn't believe in ghosts - this couldn't be happening. Nevertheless, doing as instructed, I shakily rose to open the window, and then stopped in my tracks. "Mother, if you were able to come back from the grave, surely you could come through the window yourself," I said aloud. Waiting for a response that did not come and feeling perhaps I was losing my mind, decided to go to bed, but was unable to fall asleep. Maybe Dad had been right all along…there was something wrong with me.

Gazing up at the ceiling from my bed, colored photographic slides - one after another, passed through my head. One photo showed Dad...his head fell off and then Sam's face replaced it. Next appeared a vision riding in a car with Dad and as I turned to wave good-bye to mother, suddenly it was Sam seated next to me driving the car. I made him stop the car and ran back to my mother, pinning money all over her until covered in green. Surely I needed to be in a straight jacket. In addition to all of this, depression set in over the upcoming wedding as I began to envy Shirley because she had professional help for her problems. The next morning after Artie left for work, I called Doctor Agan.

Seeing the psychologist for a few sessions I came to realize that Sam resembled Dad in a way and because of my guilt, was marrying a father substitute, giving my mother money so she would not be angry at me for taking her husband away. The feelings building up inside through the years were finally being released, and believing myself cured, would not have to go back for more sessions with the doctor. Little did I know how much more help would be required.

Sam's mother began to bake and freeze various dishes for the wedding, as I, being cheated out of my life-long aspiration of that dream, wallowed in anguish. The following Sunday morning the phone rang. "Guess who? It's me," the voice on the other end exclaimed, "Aunt Rose!" She had heard about the marriage and knew there would not be a big wedding, adding, "Do you realize you'll be the only one in the family that will not have the honor of being a bride?" I welcomed her to join us at our small affair along with the other members of the Glassberg family, but she would not hear of it, insisting upon paying for an exquisite affair. Did I hear correctly? "You will choose the hall and anything else that your heart desires and send all the bills to me." She then added, "All I ask is that you pick a place that's strictly kosher, since I am very religious." What a shock - had my prayers been answered? Would I truly become the bride of my dreams after all?

Overwhelmed I asked breathlessly, "How can I ever thank you?" She said not to even try, but to get started on all the arrangements. When I told Sam, he said it really did not make a difference to him, but felt content upon seeing my happiness. Walking on air, the planning commenced.

The finest location inevitably meant the Gold Manor on Eastern Parkway in Brooklyn, kosher, exceptionally elegant, with twin cantors to sing during the ceremony. Deposits were placed on flowers and a five-piece band and I chose the menu and selected the invitations.

With the wedding date set for December 13, planning neared completion except for the gown and the men's tuxedos. Sam had gone into the army and came home on the thirteenth plus it was his birthday. That would be my lucky number!

A few weeks later Aunt Rose called again. "Uncle Sam (her husband) will have the pleasure of walking you down the aisle and giving you away." Politely I told her that I did not mind if they were in the wedding party, but preferred that Shirley and Nat take me down the aisle in place of my parents. My heart stopped for a moment and then reluctantly, Aunt Rose agreed.

Shirley became very depressed with concerns over the upcoming wedding. "I am very unhappy about this situation," she confided. "You have no right to take this gift." My heart dropped to the floor and I asked her to explain. When our mother had needed money to help save our home, Aunt Rose had been nowhere to be found. In addition, Rose had never given back a ring that mother had given her for a loan. Most importantly, the entire Glassberg family, who had previously turned us away in our darkest hours, would be attending. "She is only doing this to ease her own guilt," Shirley concluded.

Perhaps all true, but just the same, we had done our best to keep in touch with them before our mother died. They had all attended Shirley's wedding and their generous gifts paid for her extravagant honeymoon. I did not care about my aunt's guilt. "So let her get back at mother through me," I insisted, not about to give up this vision of happiness so easily.

Shirley began to cry and refused to come if the Glassbergs attended. I really did not let this comment bother me at the time, and knowing she remained under Doctor Agan's care, I went to see him for another session. He told me how hard Shirley had taken this, and that she made herself very sick over it. "But the decision is yours to make," he told me.

I went home and cried a river. I could not hurt Shirley; I loved her too much. Nor did I forget what she had done for me back at the Pride of Judea, helping with dating and the conversations she wrote for me. How could my wedding not include my sister?

The next day I called Aunt Rose and cancelled everything, providing the excuse that it was just too hard to go through all this without my parents. She was very disappointed, the deposits were refunded, and all my joy went up in smoke. I would only be a bride in dreams, though not upset with Shirley, just sad for me, telling myself to put this all behind me. Time heals all.

Instead of the house party Sam's mother had originally planned, we decided to get married in front of a Rabbi with only the immediate family present. Artie took pictures and I wore a two-piece suit - a black velvet skirt and white blouse, plus a small band encircled my head, but no veil. Afterwards we went for lunch at the *Little Oriental*, a restaurant on Pitkin Avenue. Putting on a good show, I forced a smile and tried to act happy.

Shirley bought me a lovely gold quilted house coat with green silk lining. Artie, now engaged, he and his fiancée Ilene gave us cash. Sam's family gave us a gift of linens and a set of silverware for twelve, which were used for many years. Aunt Rose sent a set of dishes, but the rest of the Glassberg family did not send anything.

We went to Quebec Canada for our honeymoon even though December is not exactly the best time to go. We froze but luckily brought along our warm winter coats.

Far a bisel libe batsolt men miten gantsen leben.

For a little love, you pay all your life.

Dad in the Army

Dad in Brooklyn

Chapter Fifteen
Married Life

I was not looking forward to having sex for the first time, a scary concept but Sam was quite loving and gentle and it would be five days until we consummated our marriage. Sam tried to have a sense of humor about the whole thing. Attempting to prevent me from getting dressed in the morning, when I went to put on my shoes they were full of moth balls. The following day Sam had tied my shoelaces together and when I put them on and tried to walk, fell back on the bed. That led to a lovemaking session.

On the honeymoon we purchased souvenirs for everyone we knew. Before leaving Quebec, we treated ourselves to dinner at an expensive French restaurant. The waiters wore white gloves and had a white napkin over their arm at all times. Our water glasses and coffee cups were never empty, and my cigarette lit just as soon as I had taken it from my purse. I especially enjoyed the dessert wagon. Married life had not been too bad so far and on our way home I had planned to tell Sam the truth about my life, but somehow never got around to it. Maybe another time – I would just let it ride for now.

After stopping for lunch, we resumed our drive towards the United States until we suddenly lost sight of the main highway. We were on a back country road where snow had fallen the night before, and the ground had turned to ice. With a steep hill coming up and the car continuously sliding back down to the bottom, we knew we would not be able to make it. Sam locked me in the car and told me to wait as he walked to the top of the hill to look for any sign of life.

We were lucky to be near a small town, only one block long. The sheriff arrived with a tow truck and pulled us up the hill.

Everyone we encountered spoke French, but the sheriff could understand just enough English to be able to communicate. He put our car in his garage and invited us into his home.

We were introduced to his wife and two children, who provided us a tour of their home showing off all the modern conveniences they owned - refrigerator, washing machine, and running water that came from a well pumped into the house. Many of the homes in town had a side of beef hanging outside to keep the meat frozen. This tiny settlement looked like one of those Hollywood movie sets - a real one-horse town.

The sheriff's wife made some coffee and offered us plates of soft, white, curly homemade cheese. We did not like it very much and hid the pieces in our pockets while she was not looking. She was so proud of her cheese and we did not wish to be insulting, but seeing our empty plates, she filled them up again. Our pockets could barely hold all that cheese!

The sheriff took us to a neighbor's house to sleep, followed in the morning by a delicious homemade breakfast of eggs, bacon, toast, fried potatoes, juice, and coffee. We offered to pay but the woman refused to take any money.

Our car now cleaned, warmed, and with chains on the tires so that we could go safely on our way and again, everyone refused to take any money, so we left six bottles of whiskey, which we had been taking home for Sam's brother-in-law. The incident had been a pleasant experience, although we had a tough time getting all that cheese out of our pockets! We hoped to return someday, but did not think we would be able to find that road again. I think of that special place and kind folks now and then.

Artie and Ilene were planning to move in with us after their wedding and Sam and I hoped to have a child after about a year, and then move into our own apartment. Ilene had said she would stock our place with food and have dinner ready for us when we arrived home on Sunday. However, as it turned out we arrived a day early to find no one around and our cupboards empty. Sam became angry because we had to go out to eat. "The honeymoon's over," he growled. "Don't think we can eat out every day. I can't afford it." Financial matters scared him and throughout our marriage the only thing we ever really fought about would be money. We could not seem to calmly discuss these types of problems.

Then Sam added, "Whenever you go shopping, make sure you carry the bundles home yourself. No giving tips to delivery boys." His mother carried her own bags, so he thought I should too. Doesn't he know I'm his wife, and not his mother? But not knowing how to stand up for myself and fight back, I carried the bundles and avoided a conflict.

A week after the honeymoon we had our second battle. The house coat from Shirley had become soiled and could not be washed. Having taken the garment to the dry cleaners, I made the mistake of hanging it on the door at home with the ticket still attached indicating a cost of one dollar and a half. When Sam saw it he blew his top. I cried and did not speak to him for a week, by which time he had forgotten what happened. When I reminded him, he just laughed and said he could never be mad at me. I knew then some things must remain hidden from him, even if this meant having to lie.

Artie and Ilene had a wonderful wedding and I was so pleased for them. She made a beautiful bride. They moved in with us and we got along wonderfully, sharing everything just like sisters. In one year Sam and I managed to save three thousand dollars and then I became pregnant so we moved into our own one bedroom apartment on Jerome Street, just two blocks from Sam's mother, and eight blocks from Shirley.

I loved the apartment and everything in it. Sam did a wonderful job painting the rooms and our wood floors were as shiny as mirrors once they were cleaned. We purchased a honey-colored French provincial bedroom set with a baby crib to match the furniture. We bought a pink couch, a cocoa-brown club chair, lamp, and coffee table with a marble top for the living room; a washing machine and dining room set, also French provincial for the kitchen.

I bought a second-hand sewing machine and made my maternity dresses. Sam's sister Flo was also pregnant, and I made her three dresses as well.

The apartment, in a two-family house, sat above a candy store - my favorite shop. Their best customer, I went almost every day. There is nothing better than candy, ice cream, or a strawberry soda topped with whipped cream and a cherry. It's even better than sex!

Our son Mark was born in November, but most of the people in our neighborhood were older with grown children, leaving no one for Mark to play with. Shirley's neighborhood on the other hand was surrounded by people her own age - all with young children. Every day, even in snowy weather, Mark would be placed in his big coach carriage and taken for a walk over to Shirley's house. Although still not much good at conversation, I enjoyed visiting, and Mark loved being with the other children. When no one was around, Shirley became depressed, sitting and staring out the window, her house in chaos and meals never prepared. Since not very good company, I spent the day doing her cleaning and cooking, hoping my help would give her a lift, though it did not seem to help. Shirley could only be happy when laughing and talking with lots of other people. She said it helped kill the day and the only way she could be fulfilled.

Sam provided thirty-five dollars a week for food and twenty dollars for other miscellaneous spending and I shopped from push carts on the way home from Shirley's house. I liked having the freedom to choose from the various vendors that were set up all along Blake Avenue.

One day when Sam came home from work he decided to inspect the food closets. He told me that there did not seem to be thirty-five dollars worth of food, and wanted to know where the rest of the money had gone. I guess he thought I might be pocketing some of the funds, so sitting down with pen and paper in hand, listed each item purchased along with the price. He then insisted that anything left over must go in the bank because we had spent most of the three thousand dollars of our savings on furniture for the house. Unable to account for one dollar of the food money, a heated argument ensued. I began packing my things, and had been ready to walk out the door with Mark, but where I should go - I had no idea.

Before even reaching the door we made up. After all, how could I ever leave all my beautiful furniture and the luscious candy store downstairs? But it took a long time to feel comfortable again and I became determined to be ready if another argument ensued.

Mark, a colic baby and allergic to milk, could certainly give Shirley's daughter Arlene a run for the money! We took turns at night walking the floor with him. Sam removed the wheels from the crib and replaced them with springs. Tying a rope to the crib which reached to our bed, we took turns pulling it to rock Mark to sleep. Sometimes I let Mark sleep on my chest, surrounding him and the bed with pillows and chairs in case I should drop him. The colic lasted only six months; then he became the best baby anyone could ever hope for.

Mark:
I was born in the back of a station wagon...a Plymouth I believe. Perhaps a slight exaggeration, but sometimes it seemed that way. Mom and Dad were always getting us out of bed at 4 am (sometimes as early as three) to begin a journey out on a road trip to somewhere. Our parents loved to travel, and always by automobile. Perhaps that is why I love a good road trip...actually, any road trip. It's the going that counts no matter where the expedition might lead. The worst day of being on the road beats the best day of just about anything else.

Our travels were always by car and well planned, though Dad, refusing to ask directions, often got lost. Going astray sometimes led to arguments between Mom and Dad, but in the end we often found ourselves in some new unexplored territory. Dad loved to drive in the mountains of upstate New York, occasionally going nowhere and at other times ending up at some interesting treasure such as an old barn filled with junk and antiques or a greasy-spoon diner. Perhaps that is why I am a planner by nature, though not much good at asking for directions.

Anyone who thinks parents are not the major influence on their life needs to look back more closely at the past. In everything you do today, your parents likely did or said something years ago to embed a part of them within your soul.

Sharon:
Dad had a fear of taking risks, and typically this involved his worries about money. Early in their marriage Mom and Dad discussed opening a small motel, but the fear of spending money prevented them from moving forward. Years later they came close to buying a small Carvel ice cream store franchise, but again, concerns over money shut down that idea. Within a few years the location they had considered had tripled in value. After their marriage, not believing in the safety of banks, Dad kept his money under the mattress. His sister Helen eventually convinced him to open a bank account.

Mit a meisseh un mit a ligen ken men nor kinder farvigen.

With a fairy tale and with a lie you can lull only children to sleep.

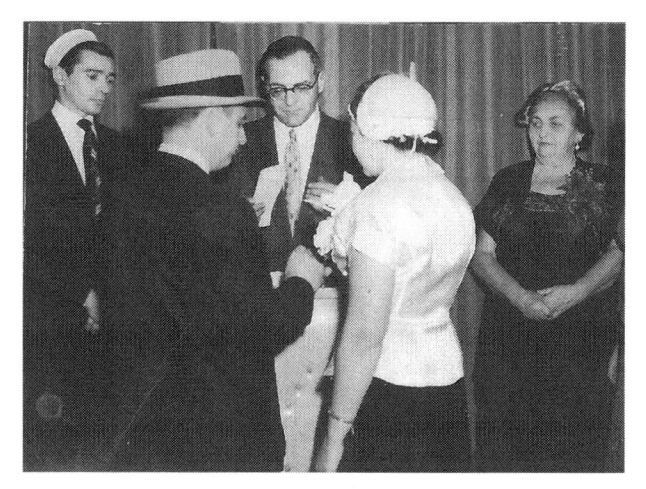

Mom's wedding. Nat (left), Dad's mom Bertha (right)

Mom and Dad

Mom and Artie

Mom and Shirley

Chapter Sixteen
Deepdale Gardens

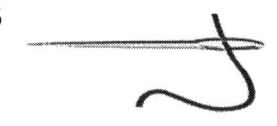

During the summer, an upstairs apartment could get very hot so we rented a place in Rockaway Beach to escape the city heat. Our place, on the upper floor of a private house, was right on the beach. We had a big bedroom and paid extra so that Sam's mother could come with us. Flo and Jerry decided to come too and rented a place of their own. Mark was eight months old and Flo's daughter Arlene a week his senior. I remember that the day I came to the hospital to give birth, Flo was going home. We were both fortunate enough to have easy deliveries, but we had looked at each other and agreed, never again!

Flo was unhappy at Rockaway because she had to cook in the same room where the baby slept. We were sitting around one rainy day and I decided to let her use my kitchen, which was certainly big enough for both of us. We put the two high chairs side by side and the children had loads of fun flinging cereal back and forth. Aside from that, we enjoyed nothing but peace and quiet - no people, no parties, and no turmoil.

Flo, like Shirley, loved to talk and be with people, dancing and having fun. She could stay up all night partying without ever getting tired. Meanwhile, Shirley became angry because she had expected me to share a place with her at the beach, but her apartment was three blocks away in a more crowded area. Sam and Jerry refused to go to a big noisy place where everyone stayed up all night. The men preferred to come home from work, eat, go for a swim, read the paper, and then go to sleep.

Flo became bored and I guess I sort of was too and our rooms were always full of sand. I spent most of the day at the water's edge, though the nights were so nice and cool. One hot and humid

Monday, Sam's mother Bertha was ironing clothes on the porch. She had eight house dresses to finish, but began to complain that she was getting tired and had to lie down so I offered to finish the ironing. When finished, hot and sweaty, I went inside with the dresses on a hanger, mad as hell to see Bertha washing Arlene's diapers by hand while Flo was relaxing on a lounge chair. Not wanting to start trouble, I said nothing, but wondered when I would learn to express what is on my mind.

The following summer we all went to what was referred to as the Borscht Circuit - a popular vacation spot for Jewish people in the Catskills near the town of Ellenville. (Borscht is a cold beet soup loved by those of Jewish and Russian heritage.) About all we did was rest and play Mah Jongg, a popular Chinese game played with tiles. On Thursday we cooked and baked for the weekend when our husbands visited.

For the men, the most important part of the weekend - sex and cards - in that order! Sometimes we hired sitters for the children and went to the Trotters (horse races) and occasionally the women got together and planned a party. I shared a place with Shirley; Flo shared with her mother.

When Flo's husband Jerry came up for the weekend, Mark and Arlene (Flo's daughter) loved to stand near the road and wait for him. He loved the children and always gave them piggyback rides when he arrived.

One summer on the Circuit, on one particular evening, Jerry not feeling well, knocked on a neighbor's door, collapsing in their hallway. Before help arrived he was dead. He was only thirty-eight and he and Flo had been married nine years. It was a very sad time for all of us. I had always liked Jerry and loved to watch Flo and Jerry's ballroom dancing. They made a great couple.

Sam's other sister, Helen, came up to the mountains to take Flo home and I stayed to help Sam's mother with Flo's Arlene. Flo waited a long time to socialize again but eventually began to date, maintaining her wonderful, vivacious personality, though never remarried.

The next summer, Shirley and Nat returned to the Catskills, sharing a bungalow with a friend, but I stayed home because Sam didn't want to spend another summer alone. The men loved to play card games and sat at three tables behind the bungalow, close to the bushes so they would not be seen - and play all day, which created a constant argument between Shirley and Nat. Perhaps the early beginning of future troubles, their trips to the mountains soon came to an end.

Nat's sister Muriel and her husband Mike had recently moved to a new rental development in Queens called Deepdale Gardens, on the edge of Long Island in Little Neck. Residents had to start in a one-bedroom apartment, putting down a five-hundred dollar security deposit, and then after a period of time, one could upgrade to a larger apartment. It was very similar to the bungalow colony of the Borsht Circuit. The houses were attached two-family units forming a semicircle court creating a nice safe place for children because everyone knew one another. On most holidays, plans were made for street parties.

Muriel and Mike loved Deepdale, so Shirley decided to move there while I thought to myself, how can I stay in Brooklyn and remain so far away from my sister. After explaining to Sam how nice it would be for Mark to have children his own age to play with, he was convinced and we decided to move. We found an apartment five blocks from Shirley. We did not have air conditioning back then so after the children went to bed, the adults sat outside where it was cool, and socialized.

Shirley lived too far away to visit and we could not leave the children inside by themselves. It took Sam six months to paint our apartment, working on weekends, and just as he finished, Shirley called to say an apartment had become available closer to her. I immediately ran to the housing office and asked if we could move in and they agreed. Now I had to break the news to Sam!

I was shocked to hear him say yes. Apparently he had been unhappy with the people in our court, so we moved again, and painted again, and became quite content. The longest phase of my journey had begun. We would live in Deepdale for thirty-one years, raising our children, making new friends, playing Mah Jongg, working, and living a typical Jewish family life.

I became pregnant again and Sharon was born on a cold day in February. She was such a good-natured baby, slept through the night right away, and just as beautiful as Mark was handsome. Sharon sucked her thumb and wound her hair around her tiny finger. Meanwhile, Mark still carried around the same blanket he had as an infant, which I had cut it in half to wash because he could not be without it for a second!

Sam worked for a builder, painting new homes on Long Island. In the winter, working outdoors in the bitter cold, his fingers became cracked and cut open and had to be taped up at night. His cousin, also a painter, had just applied for a job with the federal government in Manhattan. He was hired so Sam applied and got the job. The nice inside work meant no more taped-up fingers. The only unfortunate thing was the travel by subway into Manhattan. Sam used to joke, "I now know what a sardine feels like!" He could have traveled by Long Island Railroad, but that meant double fare and Sam always looked to save a penny. The car sat parked at home all week while Sam walked a mile to hop a bus, and then ride the sardine can into the city.

Rents were going up, food prices were on the rise, and in general things were getting very tough financially. An exclusive clothing shop offered me a job doing alterations. Nothing in that shop sold for less than seventy-five dollars. While tempted by the position, the hours were long and required leaving the children. The money would have helped, but as much as I wanted to work, turned it down.

A neighbor asked me to do some clothing alterations for an upcoming vacation while her regular dressmaker was unavailable. I would have done the job as a favor, but she insisted on paying, and unable to name a price, she gave me ten dollars. I decided to try to do some work at home allowing me to make some extra money and still be home with the children.

There was no need to advertise because there was plenty of work from word of mouth. My prices were low so I did not make much, but the money helped us take vacations with Mark and Sharon. We traveled countless roads through many states, visiting endless sites, and to keep expenses down we ate at fast food restaurants. We had a ball.

The sewing work was done at night in the living room, where we also slept, putting the children in our bedroom. If Sam happened to be sleeping on the couch, the work was prepared for the sewing machine on the kitchen floor. I was young, strong, and ambitious.

Aside from the services at the small local synagogue, coffee and Mah Jongg were the main attractions. Most of my afternoons were spent chatting with some of the other women at temple, or taking a walk to the department store…a long hike with the baby carriage. In the summer we cooked outdoors on a Hibachi and filled plastic pools with water to keep the children cool and content.

Between the job and the children, life kept quite me busy and fulfilled. Shirley complained of boredom and began falling into a deep depression, doing nothing but sleeping on the couch all day, keeping the shades down so the room remained dark. Her daughter Arlene spent a lot of time at our place as I once again tried to be a model sister by helping out with Shirley's cooking, cleaning, and laundry. Although there were a lot of other people around, my sister wanted no part of them. Life was passing her by.

Shirley wanted to move elsewhere to be near a place where she had plenty of stores to walk to. Nat really did not want to go, but finally gave in, and they soon found an apartment in the Vandervere development in Brooklyn. A woman and her two daughters lived next door and one of the young girls, Barbara Streisand, had a voice like a bluebird. Over time, Shirley became very friendly with Barbara's mother, and whenever I came to visit, Shirley was usually over at her apartment.

I missed Shirley and did not see her that often as work kept me very busy. We talked on the phone for hours, which Sam did not like one bit, often pulling the phone away in mid-sentence and hanging up. After all, it was expensive to call Brooklyn. After a while the calls became less and less as Shirley found different activities to occupy her time. The three years she spent in Brooklyn were truly the happiest ones of her life.

Her daughter Arlene had become quite independent and Shirley thought that she had some freedom at last. She took up music lessons once again - the harmonica, accordion, and piano and spent a lot of time reading, and most enjoyable of all, took a memory class at school. Another large chunk of her time was spent volunteering in homes for the aged and the sick, running bingo games and collecting prizes from local merchants to distribute to the winners. Arlene sometimes helped too. Little did Shirley know that she would not have this freedom much longer.

Shirley became pregnant and this time gave birth to a cute little boy named Barry. No one in her neighborhood had young children and all of Shirley's activities came to a grinding halt, so she immediately began looking for another apartment in a more appropriate neighborhood. Arlene was already nine years old and Shirley was not accustomed to the "diaper and bottle" routine, making it hard for her to be tied down once again.

She found a private house in Flatbush in Brooklyn where there were plenty of women with babies, although the ladies were much younger and Shirley had nothing in common with them. She decided to go back to her sessions with Doctor Agan.

By this time I had settled comfortably into my own daily routine. Although I knew just about everyone in the area, without Shirley around, did not have any friends. Then Gertie Closky moved in next door and her son Jay and Mark became best of friends, while her daughter Ivy got along well with Sharon. Gertie had a driver's license and her own car so she took me food shopping during the day so I did not have to wait for Sam at night, eventually taking me everywhere she went. We became very close and she encouraged me to learn to drive. After all, I did have access to Sam's car all day since he commuted to work by subway. It was not long before I could drive all over town, even in the rain, snow, and ice - my greatest personal accomplishment yet. I went back to seeing Doctor Agan who provided lots of encouragement. I do not think I could have survived without him.

Eventually Gertie moved to a bigger apartment five blocks away and made new friends and that would be the last we saw of her, Jay, or Ivy. They dropped us like hot potatoes and although sad, I was not hurt. After all, now I could get around on my own and there was no sense getting depressed over the situation. Our Deepdale community grew with a lot more activities and many of the women were taking up driving; I especially enjoyed playing bingo once a week. The temple expanded and adult education courses were offered.

Shirley was not doing any better so Nat asked if I would mind taking their children for a couple of weeks so she could get some rest and relaxation. I agreed. The winter was long and cold and Shirley spent most of the time shut inside her house. I told her to consider moving back by us, even offering to teach her how to hem so the two of us could work together. She could certainly use the money and with the customers coming over for fittings there would be plenty of talk and laughter. Nat and Shirley decided to take the advice and move back to Deepdale.

We were now living in a five-room apartment and Shirley found one the same size just a block and a half away. Things were looking up once again and Shirley enjoyed working with me and loved the contact with people. After the fittings were done, the customers often stayed to socialize over a pot of coffee.

Barry and Sharon came home from school for lunch and although they loved each other dearly, Sharon could not stand eating with him. Like his mother, he talked constantly and Sharon insisted he always spit in her food while be chatted. I asked Shirley if she would mind taking him home for lunch and then come back later but she refused, insisting that they were cousins and had to learn to get along. Sharon usually ended up taking her plate to her room, slamming the door behind her.

Shirley and I often talked about what would become of the children if anything should happen to one of us and agreed that the other would care of the children. To me, Barry and Arlene were like my own children anyway.

Shirley and I worked together for a few years and began getting lots of sewing jobs. I rarely did anything for entertainment; there just was not enough time. Then I made a big mistake. Shirley suggested that we put away a few dollars each week to use for fun. She put away more than I did until one day Sam needed money for a bill and I decided to take my half out and give it to him. Shirley became furious and I felt badly knowing this was the wrong decision. Ashamed, I apologized to her, but she never forgave me, bringing it up many times throughout the years.

Mark:
There is much more to the account of Barbara Streisand (she later dropped an "a" changing her name to Barbra). Roslyn, Barbra's, sister, and her mother Diane were living in the Vandervere apartment complex in Brooklyn when Shirley, Nat, and Arlene moved in. At three or four years of age and too young to remember, what I know of Barbra's history comes from stories my mother and Aunt Shirley told me, as well as recollections from my cousin Arlene.

Over the years, Shirley spoke of Barbra often. The child of the first marriage she kept the name of Streisand after her mother remarried. Her sister Roslyn (who went on to her own career in the entertainment industry) was the child of the second husband and kept the surname of Kind. The second husband then left Diane and she never got over it. Shirley and Barbra's mother Diane became friends and Roslyn became Arlene's best friend. Barbra's mother Diane and sister Roslyn also had beautiful voices.

Diane wanted Barbra to give up singing to seek a career such as secretarial work. Despite the age difference, Shirley and Barbra became friends and at the time, Shirley perhaps the one person that believed that Barbra would one day become a star. Barbra went to Shirley's apartment and acted out scenes and sung while Shirley played the piano.

Shirley told Barbra to keep singing, to follow her dream, encouraging Barbra to leave home and try to get noticed. She eventually left home and the two women did not see one another again until Barbra starred on Broadway as Fanny Brice in the show *Funny Girl*. Shirley and Nat were invited to the show and met with Barbra backstage after the play. That would be the last time the two ever saw each other.

Barbra and Shirley kept in touch for several years, Barbra informing my aunt of her many planned appearances, but their communication stopped about the time Barbra's marriage to Elliot Gould ended. Barbra remained Shirley's idol and favorite star for the rest of her life. She spoke of her often, owned all her albums (back in the day when music played on vinyl), and loved to listen to her sweet voice.

Sharon:
Dad worked hard and Mom always had dinner ready on the table when he came home. We ate together as a family at a tiny four-person table crammed into a small kitchen. When mom first married she had no formal cooking experience and Dad told us stories of his first home cooked meals in married life. Mom could boil water and prepared most meals using this method. It was after she made Dad a steak boiled in water, that he asked his mother to show his wife how to cook.

Although only nine years old, Arlene helped raise her young brother Barry, preparing his bottle and changing his diapers. Eventually Barry spent many of his early days cared for, not by his own mother, but by ours.

Mark:
Dad dropped out of school at fourteen so that he could help support his mother and sisters after his father died. His dream to go to school to become an architect now gone, he became a house painter, a career he followed during his time in the army in WWII. After the war and a stint as a house painter, Dad found employment with the federal Government Services Administration (GSA) where he remained until he retired at 68. Though not highly schooled, Dad understood the value of a dollar and he had strong opinions about wasting money. It must have been hard on Mom, raised by a father who refused to spend money and then married to a man who had the same mentality. Growing up, Sharon and I were not denied the things we needed, though we did endure many arguments related to spending money.

Our country might not be in deficit today had they taken a tip from Dad sixty years ago. A quiet man, some of his stories were passed on to us by Mom over the years. Dad had just started with the GSA and had been provided his first assignment, painting a small office. Our father, a person of high work ethic, believed in hard work with no time for goofing off on the job. Provided with all the necessary paint, brushes, rollers, and drop cloths, he set out on his first task.

Part-way into week one of this two-week project, both coats of the required government basic white paint covered the walls and ceiling. Having been warned that assignments were based on a strict schedule, he gave the now bright and shiny, yet bland walls a third and then a fourth coat. By the start of week two, Dad became bored; clearly this assignment was complete.

Dad often complained how the government bosses might have been schooled in managing people, but rarely knew anything about the thing they were managing. Painting supervisors according to Dad had never actually held a brush or opened a can of paint. A few days shy of the scheduled completion date, Dad informed his supervisor the office was complete.

The supervisor, a bit perturbed to learn the project schedule had not been kept, lectured Dad to always read the assignment carefully. In this case it called for two coats of paint. Dad perhaps made matters worse for himself when stating that he had in fact completed four coats in almost half the time of the job's scheduled duration. He was scolded and warned that in the future, a two week job meant just that. Projects are planned months in advance and what a mess it would make of things if everyone finished their work in less time than the plan required.

Fortunately the next office to be painted vacant, Dad could get started on that right away. Having been reminded to note the scheduled completion date, a list of supplies was provided to obtain from procurement. Dad scanned the list and informed the boss more supplies were not necessary. This new job specified the same paint as the last one, and an adequate supply remained of paint, brushes, and other supplies for this next assignment. Again came the lecture. Think of the problems created if leftover materials and supplies, ordered months in advance, backed up in the warehouse. "What should I do with the unopened paint and case of brushes," Dad inquired. "Take them out to the dumpster," the boss responded.

Dad hated waste and sometimes came home with the oddest things he found lurking in the government's trash. Although the trip home from work meant a long subway ride, a bus, and a mile walk, he occasionally strolled in the door with a box of some cache he had found in the dumpster. Perhaps this is how I came to fully appreciate the concept; one man's trash is another's treasure.

One time upon arriving home, Mom was presented with a box of stationery – envelopes, letterhead, and memo pads bearing the name of some congressman. Dad explained that a member of Congress had ordered new supplies, and they had left off his middle initial. Cases of this stuff made its way to the trash pile and the official had ordered another four-year supply with his name corrected. "And what are we going to do with this," inquired Mom. "Perhaps Mark and Sharon can use this for school," responded Dad. In those days we actually used pencils and paper to write or do math, not an electronic calculator or computer. Looking at the supplies I offered, "The pads could be useful for school." Dad now proud of this find, offered to get more, but I thought this batch would be sufficient.

A few weeks later Dad came home with another box of stationery from the same Congressman. "Did they misspell his name again," Mom asked. "No" responded Dad, "he did not get reelected."

A favorite story - how many government employees does it take to change a light bulb? On a typical Friday having just returned from lunch, Dad discovered the light in the office he was painting had burned out. This paint job nearly complete, Dad wanted the assignment out of the way before the end of the day. The supply room folks informed him that the building's electrician handled light bulbs. Once located, the electrician pointed out this was Friday and he could not provide a new bulb because only an electrician can change a light bulb and he was preparing to go home early for the weekend. Dad offered that he possessed skills in the science of bulb replacement, but the electrician refused to violate the rules. After some pleading from our father, the man agreed to delay the early Friday departure to change the bulb.

When they arrived at the office with this valuable commodity, the electrician exclaimed in disgust, "You did not tell me the room had a high ceiling." Dad pointed to his nearby ladder but the man informed our father that he could not go beyond rung three of a ladder unless someone held it. "I can hold the ladder," Dad informed the bulb expert. "You are not an electrician," bellowed the response. "Only an electrician can hold a ladder for an electrician." Dad explained that as a painter, he certainly knew how to handle a ladder. They did get the bulb changed, but only after Dad swore never to tell anyone about this flagrant disregard for the rules of light bulb replacement.

Trudging to work every day in New York City, spending the day with people who only cared about the job for the paycheck (at least according to Dad), and putting up with the bureaucracy, it is no surprise that sometimes Dad came home upset. He usually held back the anger, having dinner and then quietly settling in on the couch with the *Daily News*. At other times, Mom had to listen to his rants about government screw-ups, politics, and lazy workers – subjects I often think Mom cared little about although she always acted interested.

One day Dad walked in the door seething mad with a letter from the government informing him of a demotion to a painter's helper. It seems that new regulations required all federal painters pass a course on how to mix paint. "I've been painting for 40 years. I don't need someone who has never held a brush to tell me how to mix paint!"

Knowing Dad could not write well, I suggested we draft a letter requesting the government consider his 40 years of experience in lieu of the class. We included Dad's quality awards, letters from various members of Congress thanking him for a fine paint job, and the memo inviting him to be one of the painters of the White House after the election of JFK. It took officials more than a month to realize Dad already knew how to mix paint.

When the news finally came, Dad had something new to fume about. While keeping his rank as painter, new rules now required every painter to have a helper. Independent Dad was not about to have another worker carry his ladder and paint cans.

A very modest man, due in part to his desire that his children grow up pure, Dad did not smoke or drink (at least never in our presence) and avoided curse words even when arguing with Mom. So it is no wonder this last story is one we never heard, as Mom had promised never to repeat it while he lived.

Dad had been pulled away from a project for a quick but important painting assignment. All of Dad's work, of course, took place in federal buildings, though perhaps best not to reveal where this occurred in case it is classified.

Inside a small locked office sat a handful of chairs and a plain square table facing a wall covered with a curtain, which hid top secret military maps. The three uncovered walls were to be painted, but the draped wall was not to be touched. Without proper clearance, Dad had been forbidden from looking at the maps. A small man at 5'4", Dad had to protect the maps to ensure unauthorized persons did not enter the room and to be sure to lock the door if he had to leave. The importance of the secrecy had been clearly emphasized several times to make certain Dad understood. He began his painting, but as time went on Dad became curious. At first, the fact that he had been left in charge of protecting top secret maps spun in Dad's mind, but as time went on, concerns led to curiosity. What did a top secret military map look like?

Dad finished the job and almost made it out the door. He probably would not know what the maps even meant so what would it hurt to take a peek. Lifting the curtain revealed no maps, but certainly a big secret – A wall covered with photographs of naked women. Dad never spoke of this except to Mom, and one can only guess the true purpose of this secret room.

Nor naronim farlozn zikh oyf nisim.

Only fools rely on miracles.

Chapter Seventeen
Changing Jobs

Shirley needed another change, so Nat suggested that she start going to bingo with the other women and do a few hours of hem work when she got home. The pay might be less, but a change of scenery might do her some good. She took his advice and began to bug me to give up my sewing. "Let's get ourselves some normal jobs; we would not have to work as many hours," she told me. I knew she was right and the children were older now and did not need me to be around all the time. (I am a very protective mother.)

We began our job hunt but no one seemed to be hiring and I became desperate for the money. After many weeks, about to give up hope, a job came along in a department store, though only temporary for the period before Mother's Day, at least I could make a few bucks and Sam would like that. I asked Shirley if she wanted to work with me, but she refused, very angry with me for taking the job. "We don't need the money for bread," she told me. It seemed she had changed her mind about wanting to get an outside job. I on the other hand did need to help put food on the table and to use toward our summer vacations. After Mother's Day the job search began all over again.

My neighbor Elsie, a manicurist, suggested, "It's a good trade to learn. Why don't you take a course?" I decided to try, and naturally, Shirley wanted no part of this, so I went myself and loved it. The course work easy and clean, people came to the school to have their nails done. Because we practiced on customers, we only received a twenty-five cent tip, but this paid the bus fare to the school plus sometimes enough money remained to cover lunch.

After finishing school I got a job working in a salon two days a week but did not make much money, so decided to take customers at home another two days. The extra pay really made a difference and was more money than I ever made with my sewing.

Shirley and I were both seeing Doctor Agan again since we badly needed the sessions. Nat took Shirley out as much as possible - to bingo and to Jai-Alai in Connecticut, and sometimes even a night in a nice motel. Nat suggested that Shirley refurnish the house to give her something to do and take her mind off the depression, though I still ended up doing her house cleaning. Nat also bought her a car and she began driving lessons. I can recall taking her out three times to practice but she complained that I did not give her enough practice time and claimed I was mean. She inferred that I spent more time teaching Mark to drive - which happened to be true.

One time we were two blocks from the house when she told me to get out of the car, screaming, "You're not my sister!" She failed to understand that I had a husband, two children, a job, a house - not to mention the time spent cleaning her house and helping with her children. Yet thinking to myself, perhaps she is right; maybe I am not a nice person. Later she called to apologize.

Sometimes I hoped that Sam might leave me one day so that I would have a lot more time to spend with my sister. Her driving lessons all but forgotten, I drove Shirley and her friends back and forth to bingo many times. She became bored again, hence Nat pushed her to get a job. "It'll keep you busy, and you'll be with people," he told her. But she refused to go job hunting alone.

Nat's sister found Shirley a job in a charge card office and Sam drove her to work in the morning before leaving for his own job, picking her up in the evening. One holiday Monday, Nat was working and Shirley wanted to be taken to a movie. I offered to come by after Sam and I had lunch but the phone rang again five minutes later. Shirley pleaded, "Can we have lunch at the Hillside Diner?" Sam became furious, but I told him to please try to understand her loneliness, stating I would be home to have dinner with him, and walked out the door. I began to feel that I was doing to Sam what my mother had done to us all those years when we were young, ignoring her own household, running to help her brothers and sisters whenever they beckoned.

After the movie we got into the car and Shirley looked sad. "Didn't you like the movie?" I asked. She said yes, but felt unfulfilled and now wanted to go out for dinner so that by the time she got home the day would be almost over and Nat would be home. She didn't want to be alone so I suggested that she come have dinner at our house. "It is not the same as eating out," she insisted. Naturally we went because I hated when she got mad at me. Finally arriving home, I had to force down dinner so Sam did not know that I had eaten twice!

The following Sunday Nat took us all to Jai-Alai where we had a fun day and even won a few dollars. Shirley and I always played partners. She wanted an ice cream cone to eat on the way home in the car even though she knew it always made a mess when the ice cream started to melt, plus Nat did not want her to have sweets because of the diabetes. To avoid a fight, he pulled over at the first ice cream stand and bought her a scoop in a cup – much neater than a cone. The weather had been too hot a day for an argument, but Shirley started one anyway. She had wanted a cone and that is all we heard the whole way home (a two and a half hour ride).

A chapter of the Deborah Hospital for the Heart had opened in our area and Shirley and Nat became active members. They volunteered together with a very nice group of people to help raise money running bingo games, dances, parties, dinners, and other social events, and I baked trays of cookies for them to raffle off. It was all for a very good cause and they stayed involved for several years, making Shirley happy for the time being. One woman in their volunteer group soon died of cancer. Then another passed away due to a heart condition and a few of the other couples moved to Florida, ending the group.

As a patient of Doctor Agan's for almost five years, I finally learned to start letting go of my guilt, fears, and daydreams, trying my best to live in the real world, though still had a long way to go. I had not yet learned how to express myself, and to this day still repeat myself constantly, knowing it would take another lifetime to master the art of speaking. Some things are learned naturally as we grow from childhood into adulthood and I now accepted myself as me, even though this is often difficult and painful. I simply would never be the person I would have liked to have been. Finally finding the courage to tell Sam the truth about the tragedy that has been my life, he surprised me by saying, "I didn't marry your family and none of this is your fault."

Clumsy one day dropping a hotdog while serving dinner, fearing Sam would be mad for wasting food; I quickly kicked it under the refrigerator, where it stayed until we painted a year later. Another time I surprised myself when, after dropping two eggs on the kitchen floor, instead of getting upset or worrying about Sam, I picked up a third one and flung it to the ground as well. It felt so good to release the anger. "I always buy extra eggs," I later told Sam, "some to eat and some to break." He appeared stunned that I did not cry. This all sounds ridiculous, I know, but this is the person I had become - learning how to express my feelings in words and actions as well as standing up for myself by confronting Sam. After the egg incident he never got mad again when food fell on the floor or had been wasted. In fact, occasionally Sam even bent down and picked something up for me.

Sam was definitely becoming mellower and I tried hard to be better company for him. We took weekend excursions with the children every summer. Once we were in Atlantic City, New Jersey eating ice cream cones on the boardwalk when a huge sea gull swooped down and took the cone right out of Sam's hand. If he had not let go, the bird probably would have taken him too! We all had a good laugh that day.

Shirley asked me to take her for a check-up with her gynecologist, and since we both had the same doctor, she set up an appointment for me as well. She was fine. I however, had a large cyst on the left ovary and the doctor immediately sent me to a surgeon. I needed a complete hysterectomy, and was taken to North Shore Hospital. I had cancer. A few weeks of rest were followed by twenty-one radiation treatments. There had been no warning signs, and if not for that check-up the cancer would have spread throughout my body. Shirley had saved my life. Doctor Agan had always said, "She's a real diamond in the rough."

While I recuperated, Sam's sister (another Shirley) came to cook for us and help keep the kids in line. Even Artie and Ilene came to visit once in a while and she cleaned my bathroom on her hands and knees, saying, "I know you'll be upset if the house is dirty." Everyone was such a big help.

Sam had also been in North Shore Hospital recently for an ulcer hemorrhage, but I was unable to visit since no one could stay with the children, so we spoke often on the phone. Then one morning came a nice surprise. I heard people talking outside and looking out the window, saw Artie and Ilene arriving with their two children, Ellen and Steven. They were carrying suitcases and I immediately assumed that they were leaving for vacation and had come to say good-bye. Instead, they were planning to stay for a while to take care of my children so I could visit Sam.

After Shirley and Nat came back to Deepdale, the housing complex converted into a co-op requiring we purchase our apartment. The residence could then be sold for whatever price we could get, not knowing then, the value of our home, in the end, represented most of what we had to live on in retirement. Nat played cards every Thursday night and came home late, so on those nights Shirley slept at my place because she hated to be alone. I looked forward to her company each week.

Around this time, Sam's sister Flo met a very nice gentleman at a dance. He wanted to take her out for coffee, but as they were crossing the dance floor on their way to the exit, Flo fell. (The three-inch spikes she wore certainly did not help!) That ended the coffee idea, and instead, he helped her to his car and they drove straight to the emergency room. It turned out she had a fractured leg and needed a cast and crutches.

When she got home, Flo called me immediately - quite hysterical. She had a difficult time with the crutches and became frustrated, so Sam and I drove over, packed up some clothes, and took her along with her daughter Arlene to our house. I did everything to make them comfortable, pushing my things aside to give them more room, juggling work and our guests, but somehow we coped. After all, Sam had helped so much with Shirley, and now it was my turn to help his family. She stayed for four weeks and at times it felt as though we ran a motel.

Just as they returned home, Shirley began having trouble with the femur nerve in her thigh, so now it was her turn to stay with us. Just before New Year's Eve, Shirley returned to work and asked me to bake a tray of rugala (a type of pastry) to bring in to her office. I offered to make one dough, providing ninety pieces. "Not enough," she demanded in a loud angry tone, "I'll need more like three hundred." I almost fell over. "Are you planning on feeding the entire building," I demanded. After some protest, I stayed up half the night baking. The trays looked so pretty all wrapped up with colored paper as I thought maybe I should consider catering. Sam said it was awful that she asked, or rather told me to do this. "It's only once a year," I told him. Still, I could not help feeling a little foolish and taken advantage of once again.

Deep down, Sam really loved Shirley but knew that she was a bad influence on me. She went to the salon every week to get her hair and nails done and tried to talk me into going, while I always set my hair with rollers myself and knew Sam was right - I did too much for her and she was exceedingly spoiled.

Mark, in college by this point, and Sharon in high school, both got jobs at McDonalds. They had management positions, made good money, and enjoyed the work. One afternoon while on the job, Sharon noticed a particular group of people having lunch and became intrigued because they were using sign language. She became fascinated and decided to learn it herself. She attended the Helen Keller School for the blind and deaf, in Sands Point, Long Island and did some volunteer work, helping to run bingo games to raise funds for the school. I was amazed when she told me the children learned to dance and keep time to the music by feeling the vibrations from the floor.

Sharon went to La Guardia College in Queens and after completing that course she attended Gallaudet College for the hearing impaired in Washington D. C., though only attended two months since the cost of the books was very high and we could not afford them. She would have loved to stay longer.

Sharon and one of her cousins were planning to go on a cross-country bus tour, but at the last minute the cousin backed out, so I expected Sharon to do the same, but she didn't. The idea scared her a little to know that she would be with a group of strangers, but knew she would make some friends. The trip lasted six weeks and she called home once a week to let me know how things were going. She enjoyed sightseeing all over the United States and I had the summer all to myself.

Sharon made plans to take a three-week tour of Israel and her cousin backed out once again but Sharon remained determined to go. "If not brave I'll never see anything," she said. Sam and I drove her to the airport where she met up with Jane who lived in Maryland and Simon from Montreal, Canada. They became good friends and stayed together for the entire trip, enjoying the travels so much, they decided to return the following year to work on a Kibbutz for six months doing farm work in a little community in exchange for room and board. They were given some spending money as well. (This type of communal living had become popular after the time of Hitler, when people could not afford to live on their own.)

The phone bills were close to forty dollars a month and Sharon never wanted to hang up - becoming so excited as she talked about her life in Israel that I feared she might never come home. Then one day she called to tell me she felt homesick. She had been washing clothes by hand in her room, and had suddenly felt the need to return home. Sharon had a thirteen-hour flight and I was thrilled to have her back, pleased that she did the type of travels that were once my dreams.

Sharon had celebrated Passover in Israel that year while I held a Seder at home with the rest of the family. Shirley had come over to help make matzo balls for the soup, but our first batch seemed a little too soft, the next batch a bit too hard. Before we knew it, we had a hundred matzo balls on the table in front of us. "Don't worry,"

Shirley said, "we can freeze them for next year, or sell them at a stand outside for five cents each. If that doesn't work, we could always use them as snowballs in the winter!" We had a good laugh together, the side of Shirley I dearly loved, and we did end up with a decent batch to use for the soup. It would be tragic not to have matzo balls for the chicken soup!

When he was young, it was very important to have Mark attend Hebrew school. However, we did not have the money and the schooling would be very expensive, so Sam and I met with the Board of Directors at the temple hoping they could help. They allowed us to make monthly payments during the school year and continue through the summer until everything was paid up. After his four years were over, the payments would continue as long as necessary to settle the bill.

The next year we received a call from the Board and were now told we must be paid up at the end of each school year. We had no choice but to take Mark out of the school and I lost some of my feeling for the temple and for religion in general. It was heartbreaking to believe they had done this to me. We hired a Rabbi to give Mark some lessons at home and used a temple in another neighborhood for his Bar Mitzvah service, but it just was not the same as having Mark attend Hebrew School or having the event within our own community. Afterwards, we celebrated with an open house party.

When Mark attended Queens College, he went in and out of many clubs, unable to find anything he really liked until he decided to try the outdoor hiking club. Borrowing some equipment, he went on his first trip - sleeping bag, backpack, and all. He could not believe how wonderful it felt being that close to nature although not thrilled on his first trip, with the bathroom in the bushes, and a pack weighing sixty pounds. The heavy load made it difficult for him to keep up with the girls in the group, but he soon became the leader of the pack and by his third year in college he was elected the club's president. Mark now hooked, his life path forever changed.

After college, Mark took a job working in Sequoia National Park in California doing mostly menial work at first, making beds in the cabins, scrubbing toilets, and washing dishes. Over the years he moved up the ladder, from cook and eventually to management. California became his home and as of now he has been there for twenty years. Sharon went to visit Mark for two weeks and ended up staying a year, working as a hostess at a park restaurant.

Sam and I had always hoped to settle in California one day but our plans never came to pass. Now that Mark lived there we decided to go for a visit, staying at the park for four days, and Mark took us on a sightseeing tour. We climbed Moro Rock, a great granite dome. Sam reached the top, but not me. It was a long way up and even holding on to the railing, I could only make the halfway point. We saw the General Sherman sequoia tree – the largest living thing in the world and even drove through a tunnel made through a huge tree that had fallen across the road.

After we left Mark, we took a parlor car tour down the California coast visiting Hearst Castle, built into the side of a mountain with a swimming pool made of gold. We walked the Crooked Street in San Francisco and went to Fisherman's Wharf. Everyone should visit California at one time or another. The following year we decided to do something fun and went to Las Vegas. I gambled and lost. We saw the Grand Canyon, Bryce Canyon, and Zion National Parks. The food and motels were just superb and I finally experienced my traveling fantasies, though the adventures would not last.

About six months later, Sam had a triple heart bypass and they allowed me to see him as soon as they wheeled him out of the operating room. The surgeon had prepared me beforehand as to what to expect. Tubes had been inserted all over his body - a heart pump, breathing apparatus, intravenous tube, blood tube, and more, but all I could see was his face.

The next morning the doctor had good news - his body, now working on its own had been taken off the machinery. He made a very rapid recovery and a special nurse stayed with him constantly. After four months he went back to work for a year before retiring. He was getting tired of riding the subway every day.

Shirley's daughter Arlene graduated from nursing school and found a job at North Shore Hospital working in the heart department, where she met her husband, Doctor Dresdale, who later became our own special cardiologist. After Arlene became engaged she had asked me if she should have the party at home or in a restaurant. Shirley naturally wanted the latter and we should have listened to her. We ended up having the engagement party at my house, squeezed in like sardines. Sharon and I did all the cooking and baking and we had a great time. One guest commented that even if we had the party in a telephone booth it would have been wonderful.

They wanted a small wedding ceremony in the Rabbi's study with only the immediate family, but Arlene insisted that I attend too. I did not want to make waves, but still she would not take no for an answer. Shirley said that if I attended, Artie must come too. Nat, remember, also had fifteen brothers and sisters and Shirley did not want to leave any of them out, so the wedding ended up a lovely affair in a hall with Sharon as the maid of honor. Waiters came by wearing white gloves with napkins over their arms carrying trays of gourmet hors d'oeuvres. This went on for over an hour followed by an elaborate main course - a day I will never forget.

On the way to Shirley's house one day I noticed Barry helping her down the steps and into the car. She had a mild stroke and they were on their way to the hospital. She recovered very quickly but a few months later she experienced a second stroke - this one a little more severe. She went to a rehabilitation center in White Plains, New York called the Burkes Institute. Sam did not like driving that far, so for six weeks, Nat took us with him to visit every Saturday and Sunday.

We arrived at the Institute at eleven in the morning, had lunch together, and kept her company until dinner. Though still partially constrained to a wheelchair, Shirley exercised twice a day and had the opportunity to take pleasant afternoon excursions on the well-manicured grounds. Before Shirley came home I helped Nat get the house ready, working all weekend - scrubbing, vacuuming, and stocking the house with food. During her first two weeks home, to be sure she ate properly, I brought Shirley three meals a day plus snacks and as a diabetic, she required insulin twice a day. Watching her administer the needle in different places throughout her body, thighs, arm, and butt - I told myself never to become a diabetic.

The weather at least was in her favor. The days were warm and sunny and Shirley began to walk outside on her own, wheeling a baby carriage to help keep her balance. I told her to put a doll in it, so she would feel like she was taking a baby for a stroll. I walked with her in between manicures and whenever I found some spare time.

One of my manicure customers, Debbie Lerman, introduced Sharon to Joel, who also lived in Deepdale just a block away. Joel recently graduated from Oswego State University and hoped to live there someday on four acres of land upstate, which he had bought from some friends. When his father passed away he wanted to be near his mother, Roslyn, and so he stayed in Deepdale.

Joel was handsome, friendly, and very polite. On New Year's Day he came to my apartment to visit, but Sharon had gone to see Mark in California. Joel said, "I know Sharon is not here. I just came by to wish you a Happy New Year." He gave me a kiss on the cheek and left. Touched, I started to make out a wedding list, hoping Sharon felt the same way about him. She did!

Joel wore his dad's wedding band and Roslyn gave Sharon her matching one. I did all the cooking for the engagement party and Roslyn baked the cakes. Between the two of us we could have gone into the catering business. We had many different kinds of food - three varieties of chicken, sweet and sour meatballs, pot roasts, string bean casserole, kosher salads, bowls of fruit, candy, nuts, and so much more.

Mark:

When Sharon and Joel became engaged, my cousin Barry and I were working in Sequoia National Park. Mom pleaded with me to attend the engagement party, but no way could we fly across the country for a family get-together.

Although proud of my accomplishments, having now been promoted to restaurant manager, deep inside Mom wished I had remained in New York. Being on the other side of the country had been difficult on Mom, and on my annual visits, she always offered that my room remained available anytime I wanted to move back. I was well into my thirties before she seemed to accept the fact that her son would not be coming home.

Barry and I devised a grand surprise for the engagement party, and knowing how family gossip can spread, this became a closely guarded secret. We flew into New York's Kennedy Airport the afternoon prior to the event, planning to stay in a motel, crashing the party the next day. Once we arrived, and on a tight budget, we decided to stay at Arlene's house (Barry's sister) where the party was to be held. A couple of hours later we were strolling up Arlene's walkway. When we arrived at the door she thought to herself, "isn't that strange, two people who look just like Mark and Barry."

After the reality set in that the two strangers actually were us, swearing her to secrecy, we spent the night. The next morning, as Arlene prepped for the party, Barry and I took off, calling shortly after the affair had begun to wish my sister luck. Mom sounded thrilled that we had called from California, not knowing we were actually at a telephone booth just a mile away. Ten minutes later we walked in the door. The first people to see us started screaming, "Clarice, Clarice...Mark is here. It's Mark and Barry." I have never seen Mom cry so much.

My life really began with college. Before that period everything is something of a blur, although I do recall that incident with my relatives, at age ten...the not wanting kid's scene. After a typical family holiday gathering, having listened intently to the adults talk about their children growing up one day and providing grandkids, I had let the fact be known that I never wanted kids... perhaps a bit strange coming from a boy with wonderful caring parents.

The fact that a mother and father could make life exclusively about their children played heavily on my decision about kids of my own. How could one have a life if everything revolved around raising another human being? Referring to Mom as over-protective seems accurate, though looking back, maybe she simply could never do enough to feel she had done her best, and unfortunately, that concept weighed heavily on her need to make just about everyone else in the family happy except herself. Perhaps Mom seemed over-bearing at the time, but truth be told, my sister and I could not have had a more caring parent.

I attended college because that is what my parents expected. Mom almost finished high school but Dad quit school at age 14 after his father died, his teenage aspiration of becoming an architect gone, he painted houses to support his mother, brothers, and sisters. The dream lost, his creative ability to design just about anything, and then build it without ever putting plans to paper, never ceased to amaze me. I am sure he would have made an outstanding architect, but then he might never have met Mom. Dreams and fate sometimes conflict to create life's realities.

Mom loved tropical fish and that developed as a passion for me early in life. As a young teenager I became fascinated by a tank full of fancy tail guppies, angel fish, and neon tetras. Cleaning the aquariums more often than necessary, and creating new under water scenes, playing with the rocks, gravel, and fake underwater plants inspired true happiness. By the time high school was half over (a not so pleasant experience I looked forward to drawing to a close) it became evident I would indeed follow my parents desire to see me through college.

The chosen career path would be ichthyology, a biologist who studies fish, though I really did not know how someone made a living at that, especially in New York City. My parents lived their life to work and raise a family, and of course to do so in the greatest city on earth, and except for the part about not having children, I too planned on venturing down this path.

One year, Mom and Dad were planning a wedding anniversary and that meant another family vacation, except I suggested, "Mom, I am sixteen. You and Dad can go away for a weekend and I can stay at home with Sharon." My sister, four years my junior, and an experienced babysitter, could probably watch over me more than the other way around. I knew that for a fact since the one time I attempted the feat of watching a neighbor's children, Sharon had to come over and make them go to bed. One threatening yell did the trick. "I tried that," I assured her. "They have to think you mean what you say," replied my young sister. For me, this was simply further reason to never have kids of my own.

For the first time, an opportunity came for our parents to do something for themselves, not the kids. Mom inquired, "But how or why for that matter would we want to take a trip without you and Sharon?" "Because we are growing up and it is time that you did," came my answer. Mom found the concept somewhat uncomfortable.

Eventually Sharon and I moved out on our own and Mom had to learn to concentrate her life on someone else. Once her kids had found success on their own, Mom had a new reason for existing. Some people say "good living" or eating the right food gives one long life, and although Mom's time might not last as long as it should, for her at this point, making sure Dad was not alone became a reason to stay around.

No one can possibly desire to live anywhere else but the Big Apple, the center of the universe for all things happening on the planet. I was a city boy. Once in college, interests changed from biology to geology, the fish thing somehow lost. Eventually geology morphed into the true purpose of a good college education, a great social life... something I had minimal familiarity with prior to moving on to higher education.

Discovering the college's outdoor club set a new course for my future. Enthralled with hiking, backpacking, and nature, I quickly lost sight of the educational value of school, opting instead to make friends and discover new things.

In time coming to realize New York City lacked something, the search began for the elusive meaning of life. Shortly after graduating from college I departed the big city for the mountains of California...never to look back. My life had changed in more ways than one and from this point forward I would only see Mom once a year.

When Mom and Dad visited Sequoia and Kings Canyon national parks during my second year in California they were not thrilled with the minimum wage job after putting me through college. Growing up, getting into the woods meant a family trip to a local city park. On their visit we ventured out on the trail for a hike to a spectacular waterfall, but Mom refused to go to the bathroom in the woods, so we turned back just shy of the destination. As she prepared to leave the wilds of the Sierra Nevada Mountains for New York City, Mom said, "Although not thrilled about your being 3,000 miles away, or working for almost no pay, having seen the beauty of where you live, now I understand."

Mark:
Things happen for a reason, or so some people say. I think myself to be an optimistic, always trying to recognize that

bit of sunshine in the most powerful of deadly storms. In 1989 circumstances found me living in my Shangri-La, a remote spot called Cedar Grove on the valley floor of the mighty Kings Canyon National Park. Having spent the first three summers living away from home (1977-1979) flipping burgers and making beds at this location, my return to this little piece of heaven ten years later as the manager, was as good as it gets. Just a few weeks into the makings of a fine summer season, a persistent shooting pain led me to leave the canyon for a doctor visit and the prognosis of a bilateral hernia. My home for the summer a good three hours from the hospital, there was little choice but to find a temporary apartment in the city for the four-week recuperation period. A friend offered to help through the first few days after surgery, and then ongoing visits from other friends could take care of the required assistance for the remaining weeks. Of course Mom would have no such thing.

Both parents would fly to California to live with me during the recovery period, an idea not all that appealing to a grown man. The argument that the minor surgery did not require ageing parents to make such a long journey fell on deaf ears. The stronger the argument, the less convincing I became and the greater the urgency, with little choice but to succumb to the fact I would be spending a month in a tiny apartment with Mom and Dad. Yet looking back now, that hernia operation remains one of the most positive events of my adult life.

Admittedly, Mom's cooking brought back some of the good memories of childhood. Growing up we had that one black and white television, and the family gathered each evening after dinner to watch our favorite "G" rated shows, such as *Bonanza* and *The Wonderful World of Disney*. For the next four weeks, a similar scene repeated each night and crazy as this sounds thinking back now, it was not all that bad a way to recuperate - Chicken soup, sitcoms, and old reruns.

Little did I know at the time, these would be the last real conversations with my father. Weeks after my return to work and my parent's departure back to New York, Dad had a stroke. Difficulty speaking along with his already poor hearing made phone conversations nearly impossible, and by the time of my next visit to New York, Dad's health had declined. Looking back on the otherwise unpleasant ordeal of two hernias, forever I shall view that month as a lasting memory of my father, and one of the most positive periods of my life. My thanks to Mom in her ultimate wisdom to know what is best, even for a 35-year old son.

Sharon:

Mark moved across the country when he left home, while my path put me across the street, never to be far from Mom, either in physical distance or spirit, but for one exception - The vacation to visit Mark that stretched into a year. Mark's move to California had been difficult on Mom. Her life revolved around her children, and now her son lived 3,000 miles away.

When I went to visit Mark, he lived in Sequoia National Park where he worked for the park concession as a manager. Departing on a walk one day with some of Mark's friends took me to the top of an 11,000 foot peak several hours later. Having never hiked before, and now falling in love with this beautiful place, so far from the concrete jungle of New York City, a fourteen day vacation drew-out into several weeks. Sadly, the death of another employee had left a job opening for the winter and I took the position, staying well into the following summer. The big challenge - how to tell Mom that now both her children would be living on the other side of the country.

As suddenly as I had extended my stay, twelve months later the time came to return home. Mom was overjoyed.

Tsores mit yoykh iz gringer vi tsores on yoykh
Troubles with soup is easier than troubles without soup

The cousins: Left to right – Arlene and Barry, Flo's Arlene, Sharon(front), Ellen and Steven, and Mark (rear right).

Mom and Dad's 25th wedding anniversary with Sharon in the background.

Chapter Eighteen
A Dream Wedding

The wedding would be held at Temple Torah, just a few blocks from where we lived in Little Neck. It was in July and probably the hottest day of the year. Sharon wore a white organza gown trimmed with lace and pearls and sleeves that came to a point at the wrist, the dress so full, ten people could probably hide underneath! Flowers encircled a head piece with a fingertip veil and Sharon held a bouquet of white roses; the four bridesmaids carried yellow roses and wore blue dresses. Roslyn and I had gone shopping for our gowns together and wore blue as well.

The sanctuary and tables flowed with flowers and after the ceremony we enjoyed a cocktail hour consisting of an elaborate buffet of pancakes, corned beef, Chinese dishes, meatballs, chicken, and much more…a meal in itself. The adults partook in a full bar with colorful bowls of tasty punch for the children. Guests could choose as an entree either fish, chicken, or prime rib followed by sherbet and coffee and, of course, the traditional wedding cake. After a short rest, out came the rolling dessert carts. The three-piece band never stopped playing and the walls shook from all the dancing. Mark had come in from California, and some of his New York friends attended as well. Arlene danced Shirley around in her wheelchair.

Sam said that Sharon was "a dream walking" and I felt as though I had lived the wedding of my fantasies through my daughter. The afternoon wedding ended early enough to invite some guests back to our house for even more dessert - if they could fit any more in!

Sharon and Joel purchased a one-bedroom apartment across the street from us, which Sam painted while they honeymooned in

Hawaii. Upon returning, using her knowledge of sign language, Sharon got a job one block away at a school for the handicapped.

After two years Sharon became pregnant and Michael arrived in the world with bright red hair and a face full of freckles. Joel's mother wished to be called Bubbe, the Yiddish term for grandmother, while I preferred Grandma. We were both so very proud of our brand new grandson. After a few months Sharon returned to work and I helped take care of Michael, spoiling him rotten. When I was busy, Sam played with him. A good grandfather, Sam gave Michael his tool box to play with when he grew a little older. Michael loved taking the nails in and out and we found them all over the house. He also enjoyed playing with the big jar of pennies we kept and I am sure the next tenants found nails and pennies underneath the carpet, refrigerator, and radiator.

When the weather was nice I took Michael out for his favorite lunch - tuna on toast, a malted, and a giant pretzel. Sharon and Joel bought a three bedroom mobile home to put on their land upstate. The property had lots of trees and a big lawn for the children to play. Joel put up a bird feeder in the back and I enjoyed watching all the beautiful birds come and go - finches, red robins, yellow birds, and blue jays. We spent many wonderful weekends there.

After three years in Deepdale, Sharon and Joel knew the time had come to buy a house as they hoped to have a second child and needed more room. They looked all over Long Island and finally found one they both fell in love with.

Most of the people in Deepdale were beginning to sell and with young families now moving in, all those that had arrived with us years ago were leaving. The arthritis in my hand had become worse and I needed to retire. Our furniture in bad shape and the carpeting looking sad, I spoke to Sam about selling our place reasoning that if I could not work we lacked the money to fix the place up. If we sold on the other hand, we would have some money to furnish a new home plus some left over cash to enjoy. Now that both children were out of the house we really had no need for five shabby rooms. Sam was not ready to move so I manicured for a while longer.

A month later, Sam decided he wanted to move to Florida. Having visited many times I hated the hot sticky climate, but he said we had to compromise. We put the apartment up for sale and planned to take only clothing and personal treasures.

Shirley and Nat had been on bad terms for a long time, so he spent a lot of time with his sister or with us. One Wednesday morning at five-thirty, the telephone rang. Still dark outside, I knew in my heart it had to be Shirley. Nearly hysterical and so agitated that I could hardly make out her words, she told me I'd better get over there now. Sam said to mind my own business, that she was probably fighting with Nat again, and not to get involved. My answer to him, "She's my sister, and she is my business."

When I arrived, Shirley, so upset, reminded me of the time our mother almost killed our father. I felt like my mother - dropping everything and running whenever anyone in the family needed her. Had Mom done the right thing then, and was I right now to come to Shirley's aid?

Nat nearly dressed for work, was straightening his tie. Shirley said she might be sick and wanted Nat to take her to the doctor. He offered to take her to the emergency room, but she insisted he stay home from work and take her to her own doctor at two o'clock. "If you're so sick, how can you wait until then?" he asked. She told him that she simply wanted him home and so the argument went back and forth. The truth, she wanted him to retire and take care of her and he refused. She told him if he walked out the door that day, not to bother coming back. With that, he grabbed what he could hold of his clothes and went out the door. He had wanted to leave even sooner, but had guilt because of Shirley's health. Shirley provided the perfect opening, and he took it.

I had customers arriving at eight-thirty, and not even dressed yet, did not want to leave Shirley home alone, so I offered to take her with me, warning her she should never have told Nat to leave. "Don't worry," she laughed, "he'll be back."

Shirley kept calling home from my apartment, but no one answered. In the morning she went home to discover Nat had come by, but only to get some more of his clothing. Shirley regretted what she had done, asking if I could call him at his sister's house and try to talk some sense into him. He told me politely, "Not now - maybe some other time." I knew this meant the end of their marriage and so did Shirley. They had been married for forty-one years and Shirley, not well, had never been on her own. It was all very sad.

One of my customers told me that her father was a lawyer so we hired him for a reasonable fee to handle Shirley's divorce plus the sale and closing on our apartments (Shirley and Nat decided to sell as well). We had buyers for both apartments with a six-month closing date and the lawyer was handed eleven thousand dollars in escrow money for each sale. Sharon and Joel moved into their beautiful new home on Long Island, a street lined with trees and perfectly manicured lawns. Michael quickly made friends, while Sharon became involved in a Mah Jongg game once again with some neighbors.

These were good days as we began making plans to buy a condominium in Florida. Shirley asked if she could come with us while we looked; perhaps she could find a place for herself. Meanwhile, every weekend I would help clean out her apartment, and feeling very dreary once empty, Shirley came to live with us until we were ready to move. I kept working to keep busy and pass the time and before we knew it, the closing had arrived.

Sam's sister Helen suggested that she drive us down to Florida when we were ready to start condo hunting. She offered to take a two-week vacation and Shirley and I agreed to share all the expenses. Once Sam and I found a place to live, we would fly Shirley back home and eventually she might move down south too.

Arlene tried to keep Shirley busy, taking her to lunch and to get her hair and nails done once a week while Sam and I took her to dinner on Friday nights. Meanwhile, Shirley started to become angry with me. "You never take me out for a good time," she'd say, adding, "You only give me bread." I tried to explain that I was working, cleaning both her place and mine, cooking for everyone, shopping, plus doing all our laundry, though she did not care. "Nat's sister takes him out all the time," she complained, yelling on and on, slamming doors, and banging down the toilet seat so many times it finally split. Nat did not need to rely on anyone for rides because he had his own car, did not need a wheelchair, and generally capable to taking care of himself. Explaining this to Shirley appeared fruitless and even though I understood that she wanted to have some fun, I was simply not able to fulfill her needs.

Telling her she would make many new friends in Florida and always have entertainment within the condos, I honestly believed she would finally be happy. Sam meanwhile became angrier by the minute, but kept his cool on the outside. One rainy Tuesday, Shirley was taking a nap and most of my customers had postponed their nail appointments for another day. I made myself a cup of tea with lemon and sat down to relax in the living room. Sam joined me and said he had changed his mind about moving to Florida. At first I thought he meant he did not want to move at all and as my mouth dropped, he added, "I've been thinking, Mark is so far away and still single and we have one grandson and another on the way. I do not want to be so far away from Sharon, so let's move near them." Barely able to speak, I was so excited. (Not realizing it then, but Sam told me some years later that part of the reason was because he did not want to be near Shirley.)

Arlene and Barry tried to convince Shirley to go to Florida anyway to look for a place to live. Nat had a brother living there, and he agreed to help her out, but without Sam and me, Shirley refused to go. Sam suggested I should go with Shirley to Florida to help her find a place, but Shirley just did not want to live there on her own and started to look for a small apartment on Long Island. Arlene and Barry knew she would be better off in a senior citizens home where everything would be done for her so we took turns taking her to see different places, but nothing satisfied her. Busy looking for Shirley, I never even looked for my own place.

Mit rugzeh fort men nit veit.
With anger you don't get too far.

Mit mazel ken men alles.
With luck, everything is possible.

Chapter Nineteen
Sharing with Shirley

Looking through the newspaper one day, Sharon read about a new senior citizens home in Huntington on Long Island, so we decided to take Shirley to see it. A lovely driveway led to the front, with beautifully landscaped grounds. There were no steps to climb, and inside a tremendous living room provided plenty of comfortable-looking love seats, club chairs, rockers, and a big screen television. A pot of hot water, tea bags, and lemon sat on a small table in the lobby along with a large coffee urn, milk, sugar, and a tray of crackers. Everything looked so inviting.

    Staff offered a variety of daily activities and the facility included large bedrooms with hired help to take care of making the beds and general cleaning. Private rooms were more expensive, so Shirley decided to share with another woman. Shirley had the option of doing her own clothes at a laundry room, or having the help wash them for a nominal fee. Visitors were allowed to stay and eat with family members at the cost of five dollars a meal, and although everyone seemed to complain about the food, it really was not that bad and very healthy. We joined Shirley for lunch several times. Once a week, residents were taken by bus to the bank and to a local shopping area as well as occasional day trips to other places. Shirley loved her new home.

    Sam and I had to be out of our apartment in a month and we still had not found a place to live, so Sharon offered us her basement until we could find something suitable. Shirley just a ten-minute ride away, we were able to visit twice a week. We hoped to find something nearby as well, so we could still see Shirley and I could help with Michael since Sharon wanted to return to work.

I always brought Shirley anything she requested including plenty of treats – but just the same, whenever I arrived she was always crying. Her rent cost twelve hundred dollars a month and she still needed her hair done, and at three every afternoon a candy store opened for two hours. Afraid of running out of money, Shirley told me, "If only I had an extra thirty dollars a week, it would be such a blessing." Telling her I could not afford that much, offered her fifteen, and asked her not to tell Sam. This would be our secret knowing that if Sam ever found out, I would be in big trouble.

Shirley had received half the money from the sale of the apartment and Nat supported her with a small amount each week. She still had some savings left and I figured she had about the same as Sam and I. Additionally, we were all on social security (Shirley received five hundred dollars a month; I only got one hundred twenty-four a month and Sam three hundred eighty-four).

With the house sale settled, we received the eleven thousand dollar escrow check and immediately headed to the bank to deposit, but a few days later the bank called to say the check had bounced. I called the lawyer, who said, sorry, but he did not have the money anymore. I froze… Sam became sick and I thought for sure he would have another heart attack. The lawyer refused to tell me what he had done with our money, but just kept apologizing. Not even, "I'll pay you back."

Sam went looking for him, but with no luck. I think he would have killed him if he knew where he lived. We did not know what to do, so we called the police but they could not help. Sam's sister Helen suggested we call the District Attorney's office, and they took down all our information and went looking for him. We waited awhile, but eventually were paid by the *Lawyers Fund*, and a plan put in place for the attorney to return the money to the fund. Our check arrived in a few days and we were so excited that we took Sharon and her family (and Shirley of course) out to dinner at an exclusive restaurant.

Shirley started to complain that the people at the home were too old for her, crying on my shoulder, "They are all senile; I can't even carry on an intelligent or fun conversation with anyone!" But looking around at the place she lived, people were having fun, laughing with each other, taking classes, playing cards, or going on bus trips. I had a feeling her happiness would not last because she missed her family and wanted to be with us. Here I go again thinking aloud knowing I had my work cut out for me this time with Sam, trying to persuade him to take her with us when we found our own place. But what else could be done? She was my sister, my family - and my love for her knew no bounds.

Starting with hints about how nice it would be to have a two-bedroom apartment of our own instead of living in a dingy basement, and then mentioning that if Shirley came with us, sharing expenses, it would create a better standard of living. Sam warned, "Are you forgetting Deepdale - the slamming doors, the cracked toilet, the arguments, and everything else?"

Somehow convinced that things might be different now, I thought we should give it a try, and deep down Sam enjoyed Shirley's company at times - when she was not acting up. "Yes, she does make it fun," he agreed, "but she also makes arguments!" But that is all a part of life and Sam eventually became convinced.

We told Shirley about our plans, stressing that we would never leave her alone. She could come along wherever we went, and Sam would take her clothes shopping, to the bank, and anywhere else she needed to go. However, Sam would take no responsibility for her social life, adding, "I will take you to see your friends, to the library, to any social events you wish to attend. I will pick you up when you are ready to go home, but I don't want to stay there with you." Sharon added that Shirley was always welcome at her house whenever we came to visit. Months later, Shirley said I never said these things. "It's not true," she lied, "you never told me any of this."

Sharon planned to work only three days a week and I babysat Michael, at first watching him at their house when we were still apartment hunting. They had a lovely deck with soft comfortable chairs and a table in case we wanted to eat outside. The deck overlooked a large yard, surrounded by trees and bushes that were a delight to both look at and sit under. If I preferred to sit out front, a large tree in the center of the lawn provided a huge umbrella of shade. This did not sound like such a bad deal to me!

Shirley kept rushing us along to find something quickly so that she would not have to pay another month's rent. I searched and searched and even hired an agent with specific instructions as to what to look for - a ground floor apartment, no steps, and within walking distance of shopping, but we failed to find something that met all our requirements located close to Sharon.

With only three weeks left before the end of the month, Sharon saved the day when she found a community similar to the one in Deepdale, only five minutes from her house, and an available two-bedroom apartment for rent. The grounds were well kept, with benches outside and there seemed to be a mixed crowd of residents, some young, some older. Although very small, one of the bedrooms would be able to fit Shirley's bed, chest, desk, and stereo. She loved Elvis Presley and Barbra Streisand, and Shirley's record collection nearly reached the ceiling. Sam and I needed the larger bedroom since we had a big double bed. The other rooms were large and nicely carpeted, and the kitchen appliances were new including a stove with double oven and a dishwasher. A small shopping center located a block away included a kosher deli, fish market, pizza parlor, ice cream shop, card store, and food mart, to name a few. When shopping at the food store, you were allowed to wheel the shopping cart home and someone came by later to pick it up.

With utilities and phone the rent came to five hundred dollars a month for each of us. In addition, Shirley contributed thirty dollars a week for food while we put in sixty, even setting aside money for the daily newspaper. The new apartment cost Shirley six hundred dollars less per month than what she had been paying previously, and although happy about that, as soon as we moved in on the first day of September, she asked me to continue to give her fifteen dollars a week. I told her that, with all the savings, she really did not need the extra cash anymore. For the first time in my life, I actually said no to her…and it felt good.

Shirley's son Barry and one of his friends moved her things into the apartment while Joel and Sharon helped us move. Once we were done, we sat down to rest on our new living room sofa. The three-year old set in perfect condition had belonged to Sharon and we were very happy to have the furniture along with our new lives.

The next day we signed a one-year lease. Shirley had trouble signing her name (or so she said), so I ended up signing for her. After dinner we enjoyed tea and cookies in the living room to celebrate. Sam took a nap and then Shirley confided, "Barry's friend said I should pay less rent because my bedroom is smaller than yours." I was glad Sam did not hear that. I explained that our bed could never fit in her room, and that I planned to do all of the grocery shopping and cooking and Sam, the laundry, plus we would be taking her wherever she needed to go. That certainly evened things up quite a bit.

At the end of each week we divided any leftover food money two ways. (I think we should have split three ways, but decided not to make waves.) As food prices started to soar, there was less and less money each time. Shirley insisted she wanted Sam to handle the money; I guess she thought maybe I cheated her and pocketed the change. My sister made me feel bad, but I said nothing.

Sam soon went back on his plan and ended up staying whenever he took Shirley to visit some of the people she had met at her former retirement home. Sometimes we both went along and this made her feel good to show her friends how much we cared. Usually Sam either watched television or napped while I sat with the ladies pretending to be interested in whatever they happened to be saying. We ended up tagging her along everywhere, and while I only did it to keep the peace, things were beginning to get unpleasant between the three of us.

One day we were going shoe shopping and I wished to call the maintenance man to clear a path for Shirley, since it had snowed lightly the night before. But Sam said no. "You'll have to tip him," he complained. "I'll help her out to the car, since it's only a short distance away and the snow is nearly gone." I became very angry and using the back of the vacuum cleaner hose and a brush, began pushing the snow away myself. Sam was afraid I would break the vacuum, an argument ensued, and he went shopping by himself.

We enjoyed some positive moments during this period of sharing, though tension built like an over-wound spring waiting to pop. Barry had opened a used record store business (back when people still listened to music on albums) in Flushing, Queens. The store looked in poor condition when he first moved in, so Sam helped him fix up and paint, and by the time the two of them got through, the room looked fantastic. Business was good and we visited him often with Shirley. Christmas drew near and Barry wanted to put out a tray of cookies for his customers and he asked if I could bake finger cakes. I made miniature cookies, cupcakes, and brownies – 500 pieces in all. Shirley helped put the tiny decorations on using bits of pineapple, nuts, cherries, sprinkles, and fudge. Arlene took those over to the store and by the end of the day not even a crumb remained.

Mark came to New York for a visit and he and Shirley loved to eat popcorn and watch television, and of course I always got stuck cleaning up all the crumbs. But when Michael made crumbs in the living room Shirley, became angry. What did she expect from a three-year old? Shirley insisted that I spoiled him.

Desiring her company, sometimes I asked Shirley to come with me to Sharon's house to babysit. "I don't babysit," she would say. Thinking about all the times we took her to see friends, sitting and waiting until she wanted to go home - God knows I had not wanted to be there, and neither did Sam. Shirley needed continuous activity, while Sam and I often enjoyed quiet times. Needless to say we were not getting along and Shirley even became annoyed when I cleaned the apartment once a week, moaning, "It's a wasted day."

Thanksgiving also happened to be my birthday, so Sharon made dinner and threw a party. Joel, a terrific chef, a skill he learned from his mother, helped with the cooking. As usual I ate too much, but still saved room for dessert, staying up late to digest all the food. At one in the morning awakening with terrible stomach pains, I took an antacid and waited. By three o'clock as I doubled over in pain, Sam called the operator to try to locate the nearest hospital, but she sent an ambulance.

Not permitted to ride along, Sam tried to follow by car but got lost and had to go back home. X-rays, blood work, and a specialist found nothing; the diagnosis, too much turkey. After another large dose of antacid the pain disappeared and at six in the morning Sam and Shirley came to take me home.

By 9 a.m. the pain returned and this time I saw Doctor Dresdale, who thought my pain might be an appendix attack and sent me to North Shore Hospital to see a surgeon. Dr. Dresdale had been wrong, the pain disappeared again, and I went home, returning to the emergency room the next morning for more tests. I had colon cancer.

Living on broth, tea, Jell-O, and juice, I lost seventeen pounds until early February, when surgery would be performed. Tubes had been inserted throughout my body and after the operation visitors were not allowed until they were removed. Unable to even sit in a chair, it was a difficult time for me, but strong and determined to get well, after ten days I came home to recuperate with instructions to walk as much as possible, which I did.

In May, Shirley once again unhappy, decided to move to a more lively area. In spite of our disagreements, I did not want to be far from my sister, and went for another session with Doctor Agan who said that Sam and I would be better off on our own. Shirley needed lots of turmoil, while we needed peace and quiet - especially now. We could not fulfill her needs and even though we loved one another, our lifestyles were just too different to be compatible. I had finally accepted this.

Shirley found a studio apartment in Flushing in a large housing complex for senior citizens with plenty of people and lots of activities. Arlene helped her furnish and Shirley moved at the end of July. Sharon and Joel asked us to consider moving in with them and we agreed. They had a basement room for us and were willing to fix it up so we would be comfortable.

Sharon's daughter Sara arrived in May and Bubbe came to help, great company after having to deal with Shirley. Like Michael, the new baby had red hair and freckles. There was only one problem - no one in Sharon's house smoked. Shirley had long given up the habit as had Nat. Whenever I wanted a smoke, I had to go outside. Once lighting one in our basement bedroom, the smell must have wafted up the stairs. Sharon asked, "Are you smoking?" I quickly put it out. "No," I started to say but when my mouth opened to answer, smoke came floating out. Fanning the air never helped either, and I made up my mind never to do that again. In the winter, unable to quit the disgusting habit, I stood outside freezing just to have that cigarette.

Mark needed a double hernia surgery as an outpatient and he had to stay in Visalia (the closest city to Sequoia National Park) to be near the hospital. I told him to rent a place in town and Sam and I would fly to California to take care of him for four weeks, at which time he could return to live and work in the park.

I hated the trip. First we took a plane to Los Angeles, then into Visalia on a small Eagle plane which held only sixteen passengers, as I wondered if the aircraft would even make it off the runway. The flight took an hour and I could not wait until we were on the ground again.

Visalia is a lovely little town, though the temperature often goes above one hundred degrees, and did while we were there - I could not even step outside. The rooms that Mark had rented for us were lovely; an old-fashioned apartment with wood walls, a breakfast nook in the kitchen, and screened-in porch. I kept wishing we had an apartment just like this place back in New York.

While we were away, Sharon and Michael promised to take care of our twenty year-old Siamese cat, Smo-ki, who we had bought at a flea market when he was just six weeks old and white as snow. As he matured he turned tan with chocolate-colored ears, tail, nose, and paws. Smo-ki was our baby and Mark and Sharon always called him their little brother. We gave him the Jewish name of Munch and he loved to play hide-and-seek, hiding on the bed under a blanket with his lump showing in the center of the mattress. He meowed, and the children pretended to find him as he dashed from the bed to find a new hiding spot.

Smo-ki refused to eat table foods. I guess he did not care for my cooking. Whenever I opened a can of gefilte fish however, he always came running to get his share. A real Yiddish cat! Mark entered him in a "King of the Cats" contest and he won second place. No longer able to eat or drink, when we had to make the decision to put Smo-ki to sleep, I cried for days. I thought about getting another cat but it just would not be the same. Smo-ki could never be replaced, and I still think about him often.

We are truly a family of animal lovers. For a while Mark had a purebred German shepherd, but his long hours at work did not leave much time for him to provide the proper care. Seren would not be fed until late at night and did not receive the kind of exercise he needed. Mark decided to find another home for him and Arlene decided to take him. Barry flew to California to bring the dog back to New York.

When Sharon moved into her house she took with her the three doll houses and a general store she had grown up with. The three-foot tall houses all have eight rooms, a front garden with grass, two side porches, a shingled roof, and wallpaper and painted rooms with hardwood floors. The doors open and shut, and there are real windows throughout. At twelve years old, Sharon's fascination with doll houses had begun when she saw some tiny furniture pieces at a flea market, and could not resist buying them because they were so cute. Now she just needed somewhere to put them, and that's where Sam came in… constructing the doll houses from scratch! Sam could picture something in his mind and then build it without any written blueprints.

The miniature general store is Sharon's treasure and no price could be placed on what Sam had created. She furnished it herself and no one is allowed to touch it. The doll houses are surely worth so much more than money could buy, and will be passed down through the generations in our family.

Sharon and Joel's children are growing up fast and they especially love going to upstate New York to their mobile home. One day when they came home from a weekend trip, Sara, four years old at the time, entered the house first. "Hi Grandma!" she said. I asked her if she enjoyed herself, and she had. I always take a few toys along," she continued, "and leave a couple up there for next time." Asking her which ones she left this time, with a serious expression on her face she answered, "I left one very nice toy and a fart." Then she went into her bedroom to unpack the rest of her things. Oh how I enjoy my grandchildren!

On another day, Michael played hockey outside in the driveway with some friends, and as Sara watched on the sidelines, a puck flew in her direction hitting her square in the crotch. The boys immediately came over to see if she was hurt. "Don't worry," she said "I have nothing there to get hurt!" She then added, "On the other hand, Michael or daddy could have gotten hurt. They carry the family jewels with them." Out of the mouths of babes!

Sometimes we let Michael sleep downstairs in the basement with us because that makes him feel like he is away from home. Grandpa never gets much sleep, though; he spends the whole night making sure Michael is covered and warm.

Mark:
Our Cousin Barry's birth had disrupted Shirley's social life, and this fact had been no secret as he grew up. My mother never thought twice about her role as a second-mom to Arlene and Barry, and as a result, they have always remained our closest cousins. When visiting Shirley in Brooklyn, Barry liked to hide my shoes so that we could not go home. His story is an inspiring tale, using adversity to create triumph. He did poorly in school, and after high school his parents continually tried to push him towards careers in which he had no interest or lacked the required skills to succeed. I always told my aunt to let him find his own path.

His own mother Shirley did bestow on him that one thing the rest of us always considered her curse, the gift of gab. Shirley was certainly the expert. I recall one time when Barry, as usual, was at our house when the phone rang and his mom asked to speak to him. Barry picked up the phone, said a few words, and then placed the phone on the counter. We chatted a bit, he went to the bathroom, and upon returning, picked up the phone, grunted a few syllables, placing the phone back down on the kitchen counter. Next he opened the refrigerator, poured a glass of soda, and sat on the couch to enjoy his drink. A few minutes later, picking up the phone once again, he said "yes and uh-huh" and then put the receiver down again. This scene continued several times and in the course of perhaps 30 minutes, Barry spent no more than two or three minutes with the handset to his ear. "Won't your mom notice," I asked in disbelief. "No," came Barry's chuckling reply, "she is just bored and needs someone to talk at." Eventually he told his mom it had been good talking to her and he planned to be home soon. Regardless of how all this may sound, Barry loved his mother very much.

Years later Barry discovered the ideal job for someone who could comfortably talk to anyone, on any subject, without having to think about his words before they poured from his mouth…a salesman. What we considered his mother's curse evolved into his gift and he has since gone on to a very successful career. Whenever someone argues that school is the key to success, I quote Mark Twain, "I never let school interfere with my education," and then recite the tale of Barry's rise in the corporate world.

Proofreading the previous chapter, checking for spelling and grammatical errors, I could not help but think, Mom is just rambling, with no attempted murders, suicides, house fires, or starving children, her saga lacked the excitement of previous sections and perhaps some of these diversions should be deleted. Reading and appraising her ramblings further, evidently Mom, evolving, expressed the joy she now found in life through her children and grandchildren. This made me reflect on the decisions and path I have chosen. Perhaps as you reach the final years of life, it is not what you have done, where you have been, or what you have seen that will be important, but the lives of those you touched.

Sharon:
Mom grew up in a world lacking love, kisses, and hugs. I hug my own children often and can never say "I love you" enough.

L'Chayim

(A toast) to life

Left to right, Dad, Mom, Shirley, Sharon, and Mark

Chapter Twenty
Cancer--Again and Again

Since my colon cancer, I had been seeing Doctor Dresdale every three months for blood work and all remained fine for a year. Then a scan and needle biopsy determined that I now had cancer of the liver and with no time to waste, I immediately went to Sloane Kettering Hospital in Manhattan. A tube had to be inserted from my groin going up to the liver, and dye injected. The pain unbearable, and the heat so intense, it felt like being burned alive, and even though this only lasted for a few seconds, I held my breath for what seemed an eternity.

Luckily the surgery went well, though the surgeons removed twenty-five percent of my liver. The cut went from left to right all along the waistline making it appear as though I had been sawed in half. I fought hard for my life and went home in ten days.

Once the recuperation period ended, I visited Shirley every week bringing her cooked meals - everything she liked, plus extra to freeze. She had a third stroke and remained confined to a wheelchair. We enjoyed lunch together and I took her shopping for anything she thought she might need for the week. We had come a long way together on this journey, my sister's life a part of mine as close as any two people's existences can be.

Before leaving Shirley's place I always made her a bowl of sugar-free Jell-O because she still had to watch her sugar. (After I left, her neighbors told me she sent out for chocolate ice cream sodas, made extra sweet). We did this for a year and my blood work tests continued every three months. Then, after twelve months almost to the day, back I went to North Shore Hospital for additional tests which showed a growth on the right side of my waistline. This time the surgery would be easier.

Everything seemed fine for another year and then it recurred and another cancerous growth had to be removed. Doctor Dresdale said I had begun to look like a jigsaw puzzle. Then I needed a one-artery bypass, a rough procedure requiring a breathing apparatus for three days. Six weeks later radiation began - one treatment a day for eighteen days. I finally stopped smoking and became very depressed, but with Sharon and Joel's help I picked myself back up again and the cancer has been in remission for three years now. I continue to have blood drawn every three months for testing.

During these three years Sam had a stroke but therapy brought him back to normal. Then he got a blood clot in his head on the tissue covering the brain. He had the best surgeon at North Shore Hospital and struggled through. We were very grateful and to this day no one can believe what we have been through and how brave we have been.

Our car in bad shape, had to be junked. We had bought the vehicle second-hand a few years earlier, and now unable to afford a new one, we gave up driving. Sharon and Joel promised to take us wherever we needed to go, though sometimes we took a taxi. Unable to visit Shirley anymore because she lived too far away, we missed one another dearly and spoke on the telephone for long periods. Sharon prepared dinner gatherings and Barry brought Shirley to our home, and she would look at me and say, "I have no family." That hurt me tremendously but she just could not understand that I had no way to get to her. We always sent Shirley home with some of her favorite foods.

It is difficult to talk about the next part of my life without making a "gantze megilla" (a long tale), but I will do my best. Sharon's husky dropped one of his toys on a step going down to our bedroom and I tripped and broke my foot. Although only falling down one step, the fall put me in a cast for six weeks. Less than a year later, tripping on the dog's leash as he ran by, left me with a fractured knee and in a splint for four weeks. (He felt bad though, and gave me a long, wet kiss!)

December rolled around and Joel had shoveled the newly fallen snow on the driveway before leaving for work. Michael had forgotten to take out the garbage (one of his little jobs before leaving for school), so I decided to take the trash to the curb. Leave it to me to find the only spot of black ice on the newly shoveled driveway! Bang – down I went, breaking my wrist and tearing a tendon in my thumb. Boy, did I feel clumsy! A neighbor ran over to help me up as I wondered if I should laugh or cry.

About three years ago on a beautiful sunny day, Sharon took Sam and I to lunch at McDonald's followed by a trip to the park to watch the children play. Sam fell and broke his hip and must now use a walker and we are in the middle of a lawsuit over the incident.

Shirley, still depressed, needed Doctor Agan's help, but getting to his office became too difficult, so I called and arranged for him to provide sessions at her home once a week. Now eight years since we had sold our apartments, Shirley had little savings left and our funds were quickly diminishing as well. I tried to help her out by continuing to send packages of goodies and Arlene suggested that even ten dollars a month would be a big help and boost her morale to know I cared. Behind Sam's back I decided to send her a check for fifty dollars every month.

By the third check, Shirley had a heart attack and Sharon took me to see her every day after work. Shirley fell into a coma, but still we talked to her. Dr. Agan had seemed to be making good progress, but the depression and stress were just too much for her. She passed away and I was heartbroken. I couldn't believe I had lost my sister.

Not a day goes by that I don't think about her, having loved my best friend so much; and I never regretted sending those checks and care packages. Shirley once wrote a poem about Deborah Hospital, which she left for me. I will treasure it forever.

Funeral services were held at the gravesite. The coffin was open and leaning over the casket I told her, "So long, for now," but in my mind I kept telling her to hurry, jump up now before it's too late. Tell everyone you're really alive, that this is all a big joke, and we can all have a hearty laugh together. But this would be our last good-bye. Barry stood close to the coffin and spoke softly to her as it descended into the ground. We all put the first handfuls of soil over her grave.

Doctor Dresdale uncovered a problem with the blood test for my three-month check-up so I went through the tests all over again. Nothing showed so they tested the blood again. Something seemed amiss though nothing appeared wrong. Where is the cancer hiding? In another three months I will be tested again. Maybe it's a false alarm and if nothing is found, where do we look next?

Michael takes alto saxophone lessons and recently marched in a Memorial Day parade. Sara too. She is a Brownie and takes gymnastics, performing a big cartwheel whenever she enters the house, through the door and across the living room into the kitchen. They are both quite talented and I love them to death. In another two years Michael will have his Bar Mitzvah and I pray I will make it. What an honor it would be to light a candle on his cake, give him a big kiss, and have a dance with him.

In closing, I'll talk about the pow-wow we were having in the kitchen one day recently. Michael walked in and Sharon immediately asked him if he had studied his word definitions. He challenged her, "Ask me some." She responded, "What is a windpipe?" He went on to tell her, "trachea." With that Joel chimed in, "How about your butt? After all, there's no better windpipe than that!" Look what you can get out of the mouths of babes...and daddies. We laughed until we cried. We all love a good laugh. It keeps me alive.

All of my hardships began at age ten. I always recall my mother's words: "If the first part of your life is bad, as the world turns, the second half gets good." But for me, when will the second half start? At age seventy-one, I guess I'll have to wait for heaven. Hopefully there is one. If so, I'll see Shirley then and we will still be as close as two sisters could be, and we'll laugh together once again.

Perhaps I should pray as I did on the roof back at the Pride of Judea. Maybe tomorrow...only I'll have to do it from the backyard deck as I do not think I could make it on the roof of Sharon's house!

Thinking Back One Year Later

One year has gone by since I finished writing my story and Shirley left us. Where did the time go? As I glance through my story, the thought of the time I went to see the doctor after the hysterectomy comes back to me...the fear I had for my life when the surgeon said the word cancer and radiation.

Doctor Agan helped me to go on with my life in harmony while Doctor Dresdale continues to watch over my health. I can almost hear Sam growling like a bear with all the favors I did for everyone. It is wonderful how mellowing comes with time. He now sounds more like a pet cub. He is 81 and I am 71.

I don't think anyone can spoil their grandchildren as much as Sam and I. We still love to take them for lunch - pizza, Kosher deli, or tuna on toast with a malted and pretzel. I have a good laugh when I think about the time the boys were playing hockey in the driveway. The puck hit Sara in the crotch and she said she can't get hurt, only the boys can because they have the family jewels.

Someday I hope the children will recall the times they watched me write my story. Sara said, "don't forget to write in your book how beautiful you are, wrinkles and all." Michael added, "don't forget to tell that you are my sexy grandma and you should be a model."

Sitting and sipping hot tea in a glass holding the top rim with my thumb and the bottom edge with the forefinger (I'm still trying to do it right) my father's mother comes to mind. I loved to watch her pop a lump of sugar in her mouth and let the hot tea flow through, using two lumps for a glass of tea.

Sometimes I jump up from sleep and hear the silent screams in my head as my hair was shaved off at the Pride of Judea, something you never forget. Before putting my thoughts away for a while, I think of Shirley in a coma. Barry, her son, his dear friend Steve, and Sharon and I were with her constantly. We all spoke to her and believe she heard us, but merely unable to respond.

I could go on and on, but this would take too much precious time and every moment counts. Time is very priceless. All the tests show no cancer at this time, yet I keep getting stomach attacks with pain every few weeks. I eat only baby food, soft or mashed food, and liquids. I am starting tests over again, maybe they can keep me going to Michael's Bar Mitzvah. I would like to ask God to let me be there for Sara's Bat Mitzvah, but I will wait for that. Here's hoping with lots of prayers.

From Shirley's daughter Arlene:
I was aware of the life my Aunt Clarice lived because as a child I was the oldest of the cousins. My mother had been quite open about the lives of herself, Clarice, and Uncle Artie as children. My mom shared a bit of what her childhood was like with me and there probably is more that I know of Clarice's very early childhood because my mother was the oldest and exposed to things that her sister was probably too young to remember.

Unfortunately, our grandmother {Anna}, due to her unhappiness, robbed her children {our mothers} of their childhood. My mother {Shirley} tried desperately her entire adult life to reclaim her lost childhood. She was an adult as a child and a child as an adult. Aunt Clarice became an adult around the age of seven and never wanted to reclaim her childhood as it had been so painful. She lived her childhood and experienced her lost early years and happiness through her own children. Mark and Sharon were always her greatest treasures and her pleasure enjoyed through the happiness she could provide for them.

Sharon:
Although it may not sound that way, Mom hated to talk about how her sister Shirley put her down when no one else was around – even just after her colon surgery. Shirley, rarely happy, needed someone other than herself to blame. In the early years, Shirley helped Mom by showing her the

way, but later my aunt seemed to grow bitter...perhaps because her life, like Mom's, did not go the way she had planned.

I am so blessed to have Mom and Dad live with us. They never interfered and the kids loved having them close. Before Dad stopped driving, he would take them to McDonalds and the park. Mom gave Michael and Sara things to sell in their make believe store and then Mom, Dad, Joel and I bought from them. Mom loved when my mother-in-law (Bubbe) visited, spending time together talking and baking, and I often joined them at the mall for lunch. Whenever Michael became mad at us, he went downstairs to watch television with Grandma and Grandpa. They loved his visits and had become a very special time for Michael. Mom loved candy and enjoyed giving treats out at Halloween as children in their creative and festive costumes came to our door. She made Michael and Sara their costumes as well.

Mom and Barry where in the hospital visiting Shirley as she lay in a coma. She had placed instructions not to resuscitate, but when her heart stopped, the doctor's told Barry they could bring her back if he so requested. He asked our mother what he should do, and she told him this had to be his decision. He had only minutes to decide. He said yes. Shirley opened her eyes for the first time in days and Barry said his final good-bye....and then she passed.

Mark:

We are nurtured in a dream world and then born to explore life's illusions. At some point, visions must become reality if one is to feel fulfilled before death comes to the door. Mom lived her early years in her dreams and fantasies. Other than trips within a day's drive of New York City, she would rarely venture far from home. She never purchased nice clothing, although many wonderful garments made their way through her sewing machine and were bought for her children. Mom had a fabulous wedding, danced and laughed with Hollywood stars, and had countless friends… all in her dreams or through realities experienced by loved ones. There is one momentous thing, and she did it well. Raising two children, and through them, when death came knocking, her fantasies had indeed been real.

Mentsch tracht, Gott lacht.

Man plans, God laughs.

Growing old together

Sharon with Michael and Sara

The Final Chapter
From Mark Tilchen and Sharon Tilchen Balaban

Mom did make it to Michael's Bar Mitzvah though Dad had already passed just a few months earlier at age 84. The pride at watching Michael read from the Torah shone in Mom's face. Our mother never lived for herself and we truly believe the inability to leave Dad alone in his declining years kept her going. Dad had another stroke and had been placed in a special care facility. Mom visited every day and sat with him. This had become Mom's reason to stay alive...to care for her husband until the end. Dad always asked when he could go home and Mom would tell him "soon", knowing this would never come to pass. Her children grown and Aunt Shirley gone, once Dad died and the chemo no longer worked, Mom knew her time was near.

Mom's life has taught us not to measure success by what you accomplish, but rather by the accomplishments of those you have influenced. We like to think she is in heaven now with her sister Shirley and our dad. We promised Mom we would see her book published. If you have read this far, thank you for becoming the final chapter in Mom's story.

Mom at the Bar Mitzvah
(Michael, Mark, Sharon, Barry, Mom, Joel, Ellen, Ilene)

Clarice Tilchen
November 1924 - November 1998

People who say the least often say the most

Epilogue

Sharon:
In preparing this book, I tried to think back when we were kids, but it is hard remembering fun times with Mom, always working and sewing, with bizarre people in and out of the house. She tried to teach me to sew, but I hated it because my vision of sewing meant working all night and strangers tramping through your house. Mom stayed up until all hours to finish other people's clothing, always trying to please Aunt Shirley, cleaning her house and cooking for her. Mom called my wedding the one she never had. I think in her life she missed the excitement, love, and party atmosphere, and through my marriage, she finally had that joy.

She always wanted to please everyone else, and unfortunately, I inherited that trait from her. There are things that I do or say that are just like Mom. It took me many years to learn not to make others my priority. Of course, I still do this for my kids, buying for them before myself. I will do without just like Mom.

Things got tougher when Mom and Dad were both in and out of the hospital. At first, it was one at a time, then Dad with hip surgery and stroke and Mom with another cancer surgery. A couple of times they were both in different hospitals - Dad in Port Jefferson for rehab and Mom at North Shore for one of her cancer surgeries. It became awfully stressful.

When Dad went to Gurwin nursing home, I dropped Mom off every day and she stayed with him for hours. Sometimes we took him out for lunch and he loved when the kids came and brought him candy. Mom had several surgeries over a ten year period, but the cancer always came back in a different area. At one point she went more than 3 years cancer free and we thought she was clean. I took Mom for blood work to Dr. Dresdale every 3 months, and the final cancer phase started in the colon, then about a year later, the liver, and finally her stomach.

I remember one night waking up about 3 am and perceived someone staring at me. Mom stood in the doorway of our bedroom not wanting to arouse us, she just waited hoping we would wake up. She experienced so much pain; we had to take her to the emergency room, sometimes bringing her home from the hospital and then back again that same day or the next because of the pain. I cry now thinking back.

Toward the end it became even more stressful and emotional with Mom eventually given chemo when the cancer spread and no more surgery could be done. The first chemo didn't work, they changed it, and that is when her hair fell out. Joel dropped her at North Shore Hospital in the morning on his way to work, and I picked her up after work.

Before she died she was in North Shore Hospital and they said nothing more could be done so she was placed in a hospice in the Bronx. They told me she had 3 to 6 months and Mom agreed to go, but then panic set in because she knew she would not be coming home again. I was in such denial as well. When we visited, the illness affected her mind, and as I pushed her around by the window in a wheelchair, she would be grabbing for something, trying to collect the garbage she thought she saw. After a while, she remained sedated.

I told the doctor when I returned the next day, I wanted to be able to talk to her, but upon arrival with Joel and the kids, I knew why they kept her drugged. The cancer had gone to her brain and she kept trying to pull the IV out and take her clothes off thinking bugs covered her body. The call came at 3 am. She died one week after we placed her in the hospice.

I have been thinking about Mom and Dad a lot lately, usually getting like this around the holidays. Joel and I often went into the city on Christmas Day just like similar excursions with Mom and Dad when we were young to see the wonderful holiday store displays and the magnificent Christmas tree and ice skaters at

Rockefeller Center. Sometimes we do the Jewish Christmas Day thing and go the movies. Recently my employer started a "Day of Giving" and we feed the homeless, a great way to give back and feel good about who we are...an important lesson Mom has taught us over the years.

Mark:

Mom passed just before Thanksgiving. She went fast. Sharon had already bought the turkey and fixing, for what should have been another traditional family gathering. The mourners and well-wishes gone, Sharon wondered what we should do about Thanksgiving. We decided this holiday is about giving thanks...about celebrating life. The family, my niece, and nephew needed to understand that death is our opportunity to celebrate life. Being with family in rejoice, is a time to commemorate those who have made us who we are and this Thanksgiving became the chance to show our appreciation for all that Mom had meant to so many.

Mom protected me, even if just in spirit since I lived 3,000 miles away. At the funeral, watching relatives and friends toss shovels of soil on to her coffin deep in the ground, the realization hit that life's burdens were now mine alone to bare. Mom was gone. If you, the reader, have parents living far away, call them today. Visit them as often as you can because once a year will one day seem like it had not been often enough.

A significant portion of my life has been spent searching for the meaning of life. I never thought much about whether a heaven might exist, instead living each day in pursuit of something, although I knew not what that might be. Having read Mom's story, I sure hope there is a heaven so that I can one day share with her all the things I wish I could now say. And if there is a store in heaven I will be sure to bring her a doll and some candy. For now, I will simply look up and hope she still loves to read.

History tells us no one has yet to get out of this world alive. The odds are anyone reading these words will follow that path.

Knowing this, perhaps the best we can do is leave behind a legacy, a bequest that touches people, that changes people, that sets a positive course for someone's future. One person can do that. Our mother did that. Mom originally titled her story *Blame it on Anna: My Life of Hardship and Tragedy Thanks to my Mother*, but Sharon and I thought the title sounded a bit long, but more significant, this is not a story of hardship and tragedy, but rather one of happiness and triumph.

As an adult, I moved across the country while Sharon headed across the street. Growing old may seem difficult or scary, but sharing the journey with loved ones, as Mom did with her sister, makes for a spirited adventure. Mom has finally taught me so many years later; this is what family is all about. I guess that is a lesson Sharon has known all along.

Sharon and Mark:
When Mom died we hope she finally found happiness, looking down from heaven, knowing she had made the world a better place for so many. Hopefully she is pleased that we kept the promise to publish her book.

What could be a greater accomplishment than having given everything you have within yourself, never expecting anything in return? Not a thank you, a kiss or even a hug, but rather simply the knowledge you have given with love.

Time flies so fast and we must wonder if one's life can really be summed up in a few chapters of a book. It makes us speculate how long "our book" will be. Perhaps we need to do more of everything so that the story fills at least a couple of volumes. Some things we remember like they were yesterday, while others feel like they are a piece of someone else's life. We were not around of course when Mom met Dad, and regardless of the challenges Mom faced during her marriage, how lucky we were for that event.

This was Mom's story, and now ours as well. It took us several years to get her scribbled words into book format. Mom's story has reminded us of all the essential lessons learned over the years. Of the importance of family and the need to let go when no other option exists. The need to know you have found life's joy and serenity when your story reaches its end. We hope for Mom, it is her story finally told.

"It is never too late to be who you might have been." George Elliot

Oyb ich leb'n, ich oyt zayn ir Montik, oyb nayt, Dinstik.

If I live, I'll see you Monday, if not, Tuesday.

In Memory of...

As this book was nearing completion our Uncle Artie passed away. Although a quiet person like Mom, our uncle always had insightful words of wisdom to impart on his nieces and nephews. We hope that he is in a better place, sharing something special with his two sisters.

A few weeks later, our beloved cousin Barry died unexpectedly at the age of 50. Barry lived every day as if it was his best day. In this crazy stressful world, we can only assume God needed someone to brighten his day.

Mark and Sharon

About the Authors

Sharon Tilchen Balaban lives on Long Island with her husband Joel. They have two adult children, Michael and Sara.

Mark Tilchen resides in California with his wife Kristi, with whom he shares her two grown children, Dustin and Brandi. He finally had the chance to experience the joy his mother had in being a parent.

Clarice Tilchen dwells in Heaven with her sister and husband, but her soul lies here on Earth within her children and grandkids.

You may write the authors at **blameanna@gmail.com** or through Clarice Tilchen's website at **http://blameitonanna.weebly.com**